# Snowball Launchers, Giant-Pumpkin Growers,

*and other*



# COOL CONTRAPTIONS

**TOM FOX**

STERLING PUBLISHING CO., INC.
NEW YORK

Illustrated by Joel Holland
Designed by Kelly Blair
Edited by Claire Bazinet

**Library of Congress Cataloging-in-Publication Data**
Fox, Tom (Thomas R.)
Snowball launchers, giant-pumpkin growers, and other cool contraptions/Tom Fox.
p. cm.
Includes index.
ISBN-13: 978-0-8069-5515-5
ISBN-10: 0-8069-5515-5
1. Handicraft—Juvenile literature. I. Title.

TT160.F635 2006
745.5—dc22

2005032781

10 9 8 7 6 5 4 3 2 1

Published by Sterling Publishing Co., Inc.
387 Park Avenue South, New York, NY 10016

Distributed in Canada by Sterling Publishing
c/o Canadian Manda Group, 165 Dufferin Street
Toronto, Ontario, Canada M6K 3H6
Distributed in the United Kingdom by GMC Distribution Services
Castle Place, 166 High Street, Lewes, East Sussex, England BN7 1XU
Distributed in Australia by Capricorn Link (Australia) Pty. Ltd.
P.O. Box 704, Windsor, NSW 2756, Australia

*Printed in China*


Sterling ISBN-13: 978-0-8069-5515-5
ISBN-10: 0-8069-5515-5

For information about custom editions, special sales, premium and
corporate purchases, please contact Sterling Special Sales
Department at 800-805-5489 or specialsales@sterlingpub.com.

# CONTENTS

## TURN SIMPLE STUFF INTO COOL CONTRAPTIONS

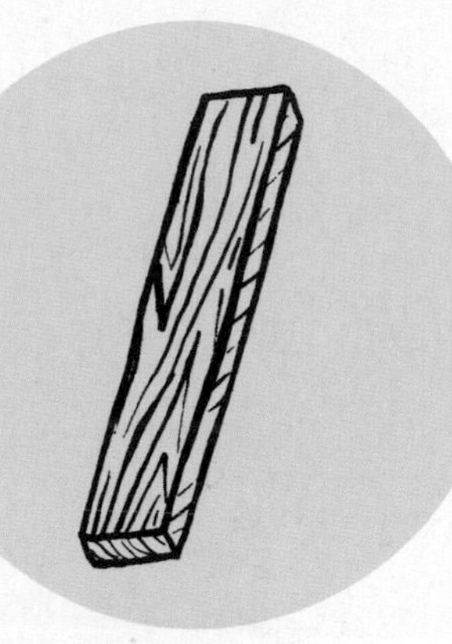

Do you have secret things you'd like to keep away from the prying eyes and curious hands of little brothers and sisters? Would you like to grow pumpkins so big that you, or maybe even your mom or dad, can't lift them? Are you looking for the perfect place to show off special rocks, coins, and other cool stuff? Does your arm get tired and start hurting right in the middle of a snowball fight? Would you like to look up and see stars, even on cold nights while you are snuggled up in your warm bed? Are you bored with having to feed your cat or dog every day?

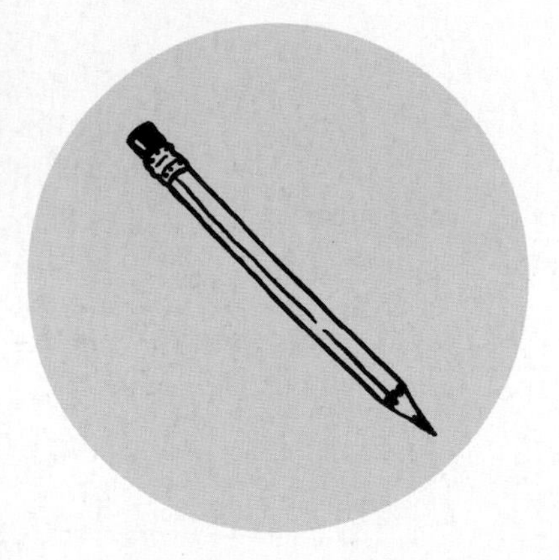

If you answered yes to any of these questions, you'll find that this book is a very valuable guide. There are projects here that will solve these problems—and more—for you. If you are fascinated by robotics, you'll certainly want to make Moth-Bot, which moves eerily toward light all by itself. If hiking is your style, you can be the first kid on your block to make an accurate solar-powered pocket watch—out of wood!

Other interesting and useful projects include a device that allows you to view solar eclipses and even sunspots without damaging your eyes; a stethoscope like the one your doctor has, so you can listen to your own and your friends' heartbeats; an electromagnet; a Morse Code-type telegraph; and a thingama-jig that actually detects invisible light! So let's get started. But first, let's go over a few basics about building things.

# ABOUT BUILDING THINGS

## WOOD BOARDS

Many of the projects in this book use wood boards. Wood boards are sold by size (thickness and width), but the actual dimensions are smaller than you would think. Say you buy an 8' piece of board called a two-by-four. Yes, the board will be 8' long, but it will only be 1½" thick by 3½" wide—not 2 by 4. The same goes for a 1 by 6 size; the board will actually be ¾" thick by 5½" wide, not 1" by 6". Here's a list of lumber names and their actual dimensions:

Measurements
" = inch or inches
' = foot or feet

| Lumber (name) | Actual Size (inches) |
| --- | --- |
| 2 × 4 (two-by-four) | 1½" × 3½" |
| 1 × 2 (one-by-two) | ½" × 1½"* |
| 1 × 4 (one-by-four) | ¾" × 3½" |
| 1 × 6 (one-by-six) | ¾" × 5½" |
| 1 × 8 (one-by-eight) | ¾" × 7½" |

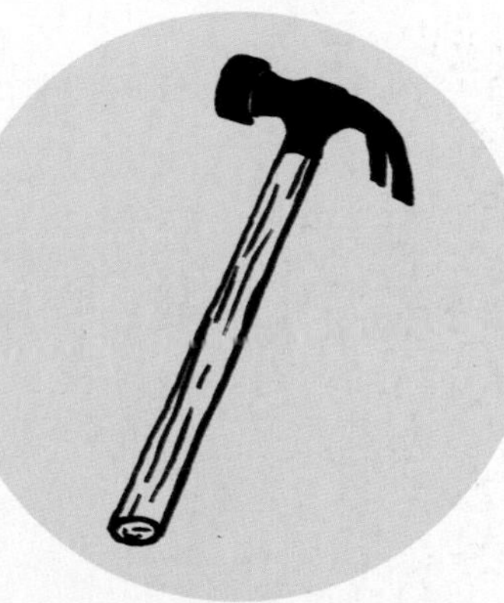

*Size varies; and one-by-two board is not available everywhere.

When buying lumber, you need to specify both the size and the grade of the boards you want. Grades are generally designated "clear" (the best), A#1 (A number 1), A#2, A#3, and A#4. While the clear and A#1 grades are best, they're so expensive that I don't recommend them. Grade A#4 is often quite inferior, though, so unless you are able to hand-select usable A#4 boards from a pile, I suggest using A#2 or A#3.

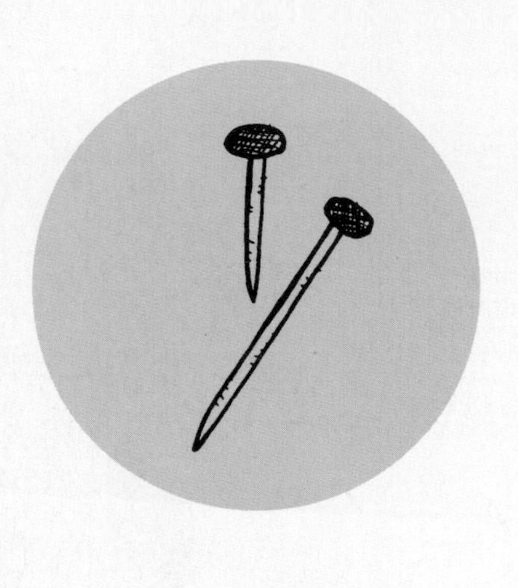

## NAILS

Nails come in all types and sizes. Generally, we will be using standard "common coated" nails, and these range in size from 4d to 20d. The larger the number, the larger the nail. Note: The word "penny" is often used instead of "d" when referring to nails, so if you want 8d-size nails, ask the salesperson for "eightpenny" nails.

## SCREWS

Two types of screws are used in the book—wood and machine. Both screws come in a wide range of thicknesses and lengths. They also come with several different types of heads—usually flat or round.

Machine screws are almost always used with the same types of nuts. An example of a machine screw is the "6-32". Here the "6" refers to the size (diameter) of the screw (about ⅛") and the "32" the number of threads per inch. The larger the first number (6 in our example) the larger the screw and the larger the second number the finer the threads. Thus a "10-24" screw is thicker than a "6-32" but it has only 24 threads per inch. A 24 threads per inch screw is said to be a "coarser" threaded screw than a 32 threads per inch screw. The nut must be the exact same size and threading as the screw in order to work right.

Wood screws are similar but they are usually pointed and, since they are meant to go into wood, a nut is never used. Also, the number of threads per inch are seldom mentioned so don't worry about them. Usually, a pilot hole, smaller than the diameter of the screw, is drilled into the wood before you put the screw in the wood. However, with softer wood, sometimes a pilot hole isn't necessary. In this case, all you need to do is make a little starter hole with a small nail. Most but not all the screws used in the book are either #6 or #8.

## WHERE TO GET STUFF TO MAKE THINGS

Many of these projects are made up of things that are normally thrown out or recycled, such as cardboard boxes and cylinders, jar lids, and lots of ice-cream-bar sticks. Other small building materials can be picked up inexpensively at your local hardware or home furnishings store or lumberyard. If you are lucky enough to have relatives or good friends who are into building things, you may be able to get much of what you need from them. Remember, always ask politely.

Unfortunately, people don't often throw out or recycle electrical or electronic stuff, so finding the makings for projects that use these materials could be difficult. Your local electronics store will sell most of what you need, and parts can always be ordered through mail order or Internet electronic-parts stores.

ROCKET-PROPELLED
TOY CAR
Project 1

Rockets are fun! Rockets are fascinating! They conjure up images of space travel, journeys to the stars, visits to distant planets, discovery of new worlds. But how does a rocket move? To explore the fascinating world of rocket propulsion, let's build a rocket-propelled toy car. This one is easy to make and fun to use.

## WHAT YOU NEED

- one medium-sized balloon
- one plastic straw
- several rubber bands
- a few feet of string
- one small toy car*

*The car can be one you've made out of interlocking plastic building blocks or other materials, with wheels that move easily.

# 1 MAKING IT

1. To make your Rocket-Propelled Toy Car, blow up a medium-sized balloon a few times to stretch and prime it.
2. Stick one end of a plastic straw into the balloon's opening. Stick the straw in quite far, but make sure that at least 3" of the straw are sticking out.
3. Using rubber bands, attach the balloon's end tightly to the straw. Twist the rubber bands snugly around the balloon and straw so air can escape only through the straw.
4. Finally, using more rubber bands or some string, attach the balloon and straw to the car, being sure that the rubber bands or string don't prevent the wheels from turning. The straw should be pointing to the back of the car. See **Fig. 1**.

# 2 TRYING IT OUT

Blow hard on the end of the straw to inflate the balloon. Once the balloon is blown up enough, pinch the end of the straw so air doesn't escape. Put the car down on a hard surface and let go of the straw. The car should move. How fast it moves depends on how much you have blown up the balloon and how heavy the car is. To make the car go faster, you might want to try two or three straws in a balloon. To make the car go farther, use only one straw and a larger balloon.

The drinking straw is held to the "car" with rubber bands or string.

Attach the balloon and straw to a toy car or a base made with plastic bricks or other building blocks. Note: Designs can vary widely.

Place one end of the drinking straw into the balloon and use small rubber bands to tighten the balloon opening around the straw.

**Fig. 1**

## WHY DOES THE CAR MOVE?

The answer to this question is well understood today. However, before English physicist and mathematician Sir Isaac Newton published his important work on gravity and gravitation (Principia, 1687), it was a mystery to most people. It still may be surprising to learn that it's not the air rushing out of the straw that causes the car to move. What does it, then? It is the pressurized air still in the balloon!

To explain this a little more clearly, look at **Fig. 2.** It shows a simple long cylinder with pressurized air inside. Notice that the air, shown by the arrows, is pushing equally in all directions. It is pushing to the right just as hard as it is pushing to the left, so the cylinder doesn't move. Try pushing your right hand up against your left with equal force. Neither hand moves, right?

Now look at **Fig. 3.** The left wall of the cylinder is suddenly gone. Until all the pressurized air leaves the cylinder, a force still pushes to the right. With the left wall removed, the force pushing left has nothing to push against, and the air shoots out. If the cylinder were on wheels, it would move to the right. Why? Because there is still a force pushing to the right but not the left. Put your two hands together again. This time push really hard with your left hand against your right, but don't push back with your right hand. What happens? Your left hand pushes your right hand toward the right. This is the reason your rocket-propelled car moves forward. The only real difference is that with the rocket-propelled car there is only a small hole in the straw. With the cylinder in **Fig. 3**, there is a large hole—the entire left wall is gone. But essentially, the small hole in the straw and the large hole in the cylinder do the same job.

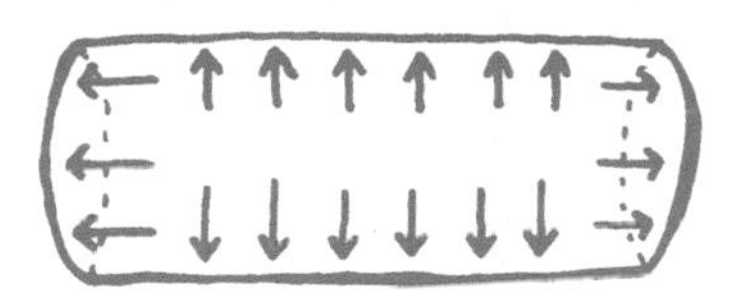

**Fig. 2**

The arrows represent air pressure pushing on the sides of a sealed container. Forces are equal in all directions, so no movement occurs.

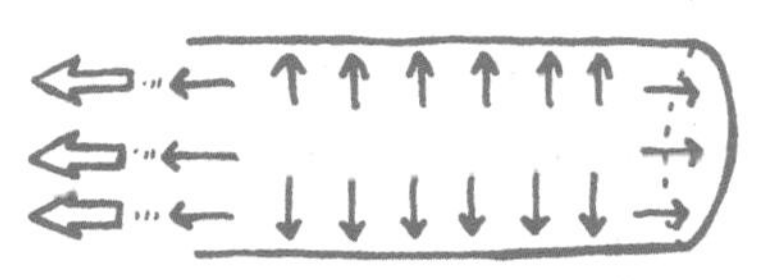

**Fig. 3**

With the left wall of the cylinder removed, the pressurized air in the cylinder can push only to the right, because there is nothing on the left to push against. (If the cylinder were on wheels, it would move to the right.) The arrows shown on the left indicate air that will shoot out of the cylinder until the air pressure in the cylinder disappears.

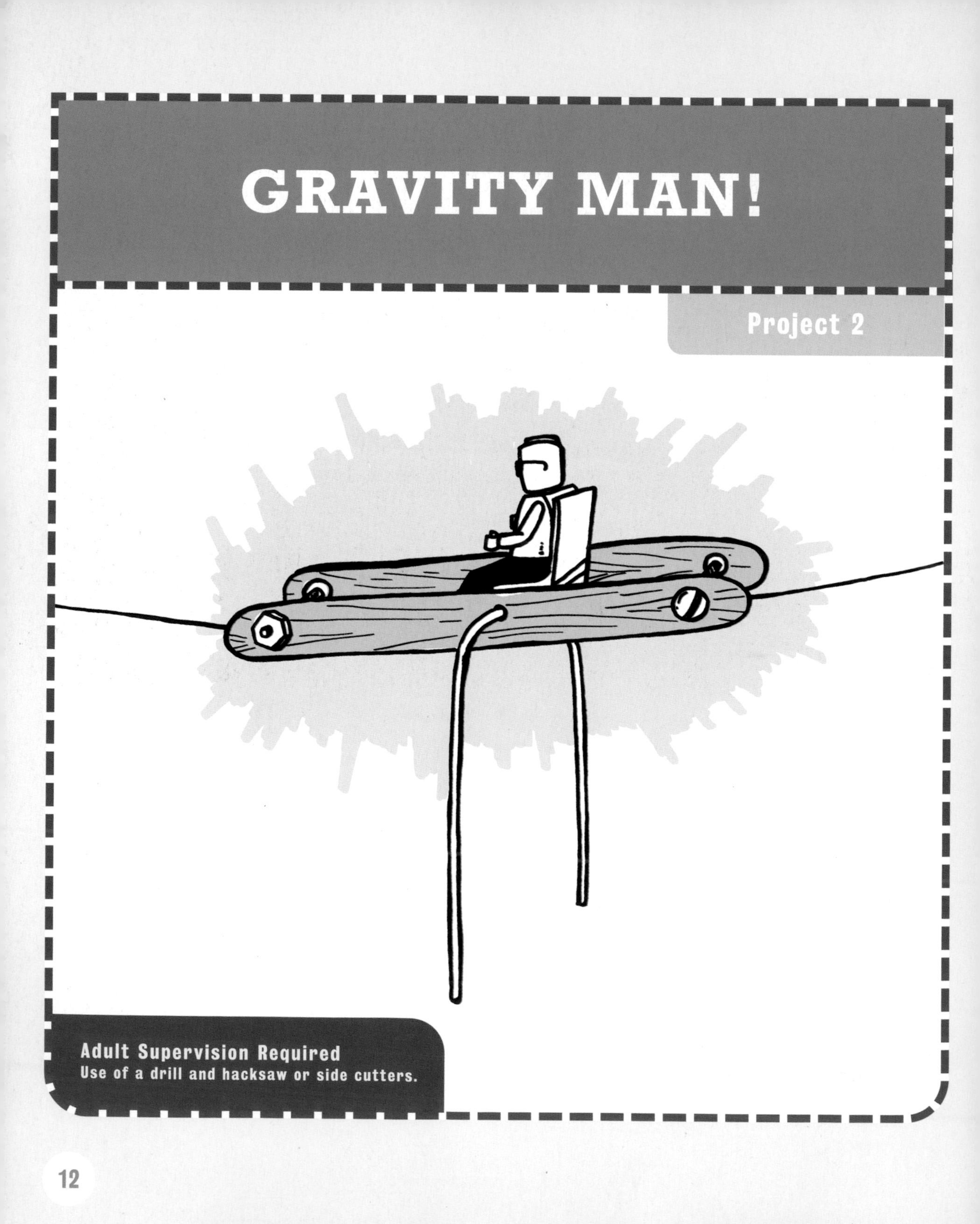
GRAVITY MAN!
Project 2
Adult Supervision Required
Use of a drill and hacksaw or side cutters.

Isaac Newton may have "discovered" gravity when he saw an apple fall from a tree, but he really didn't understand what he had discovered. To Newton, gravity remained pretty much a mystery. Albert Einstein may have added to the knowledge of gravity's effects when he published his General Theory of Relativity, but other than thinking of gravity as "warped space," people still considered it a mystery. What gravity actually is, in fact, is still a mystery, even to scientists who have studied it all their lives. Explore the fun of the mystery called gravity with this small, two-wheeled, antigravity car that can "mysteriously" travel down a taut kite string in midair without falling off! It'll mystify your friends for sure!

## WHAT YOU NEED

- two craft (ice-cream-pop) sticks
- two 1" 6-32 machine screws
- six 6-32 nuts
- four #10 metal washers (about 2" in diameter)
- two #6 metal washers (about 3⁄16" in diameter)
- one metal coat hanger (or other heavy wire)
- kite or other strong string
- small interlocking plastic building blocks (optional)

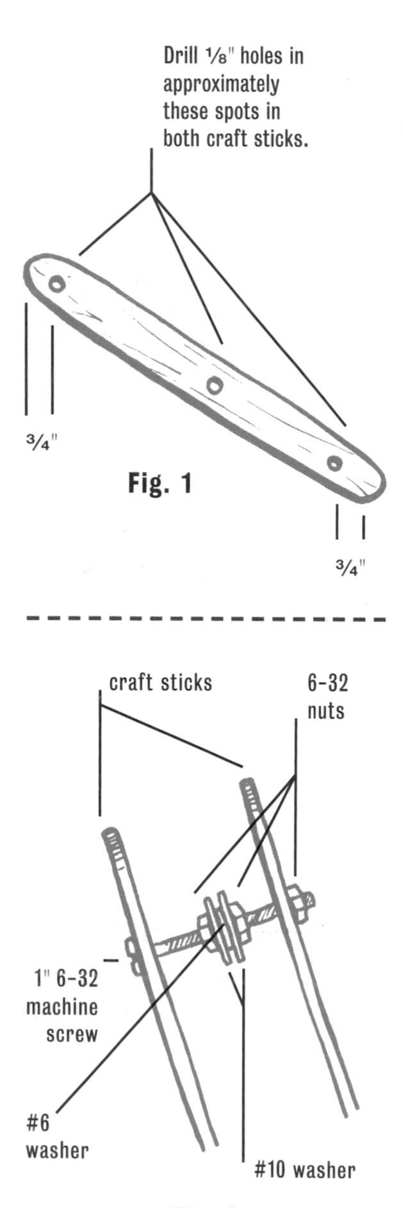

Fig. 1

Fig. 2
Close-up View of One Slider

## 1 MAKING IT

1. First drill 1/8" holes in the craft sticks (the sliders), as shown in **Fig. 1**. The exact location of the holes isn't critical: **Fig. 1** is given only as a guide.
2. Following the close-up of one end of the slider, shown in **Fig. 2**, push a machine screw into one of the drilled holes of one of the craft sticks. Install the nuts and washers as shown in **Fig. 2**.
3. Attach a second craft stick to the first one by inserting the end of the screw you already passed through the hole in the first stick into one of the second stick's outside holes and then screwing on a nut.
4. Similarly, install a screw, nuts, and washers in the holes on the other end of the craft sticks. See **Fig. 1** and **Fig. 2**. The two screws point in opposite directions. This is done to help balance the car. To make the "mystery" car that will run on a tight string even more fun to play with, add a chair and seated figure made of interlocking plastic building blocks. Tighten the nuts on the screws to keep them in place (see **Fig. 3**).

## 2 TRYING IT OUT

Tie a kite string across a room about 4' off the floor. Make sure the string is tight and one end is about 2' higher than the other. Place the car carefully on the high portion of the string so that it rests in the groove made by the washers. Let it go! What happens? It falls to the ground, right? Now, you may think it's impossible for a two-wheeled car whose wheels don't turn to stay on a thin little string. You are wrong! Making use of the mystery of gravity will do the trick!

## 3 ADDING THE MYSTERY OF GRAVITY

Use a hacksaw or side cutters to cut off the bottom section of a coat hanger. Stick the wire from the coat hanger through the center holes of the sticks. An equal amount of wire should stick out on both ends. Bend each end of the wire downward as far as possible. Now try to run the car on the kite string as you did before. You will be pleasantly surprised!

**Fig. 3**

Assembled mystery car ready for testing. Add chair and figure made from plastic bricks if desired. Notice center holes in sliders for insertion of coat-hanger wire.

## HOW DOES IT WORK?

Why does the car fall off the string without the coat-hanger wire while it easily stays on the string with it? The principle here is called the "center of gravity." What happens is that the wire, when the ends are bent downward, makes gravity "think" the center of the car is directly below the string, and so the car doesn't have the force of gravity pulling it off, just pulling it down. Before the wire was added, the center of gravity was above the string, so the car easily fell off. While scientists understand and use the term "center of gravity," that doesn't mean they have solved the mystery of gravity. It simply means that they know what gravity does and can make it do some seemingly amazing things!

# HEARTBEAT MONITOR

(Pssst! It also lets you hear whispering behind closed doors!)

Project 3

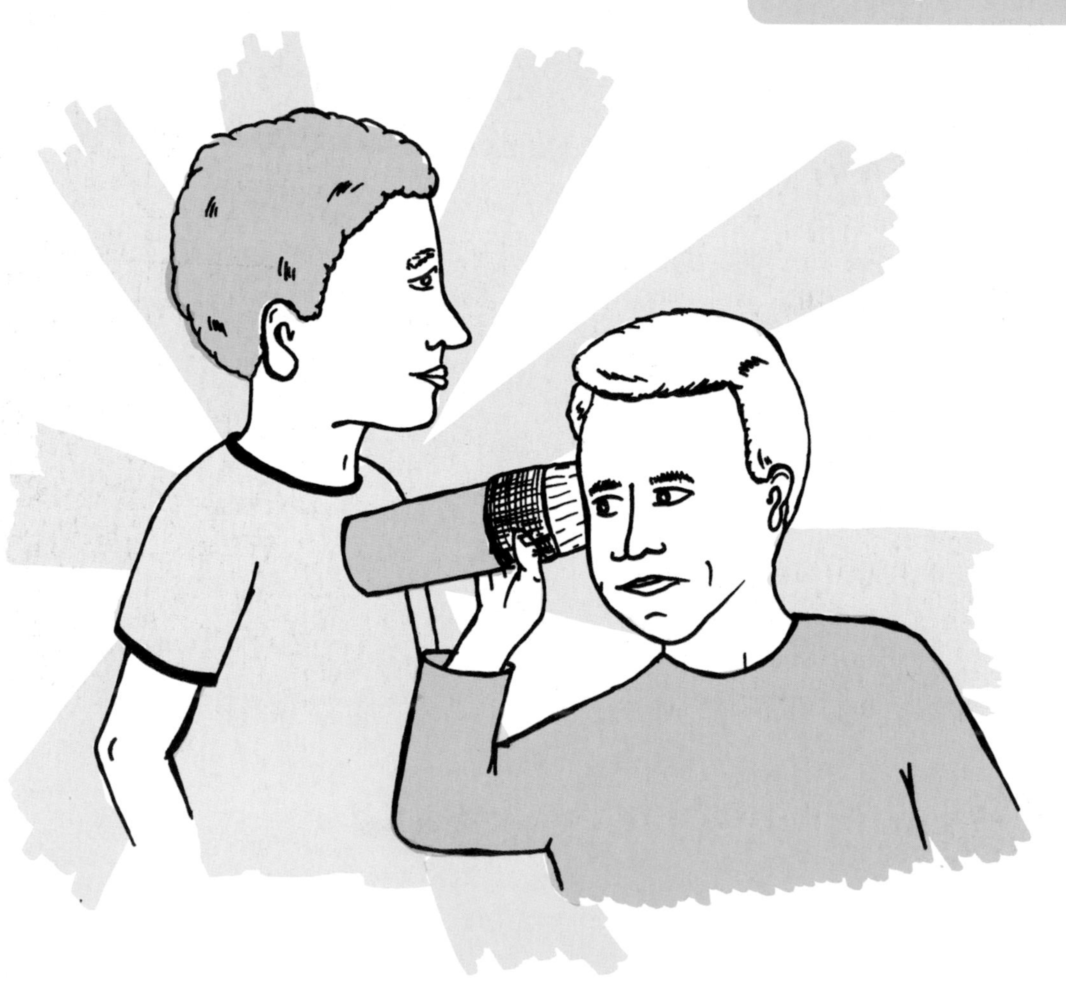

When you go for a check-up, the doctor often uses an instrument to listen to your heart and lungs. The gadget the doctor uses is a stethoscope. It seems that the first stethoscope was simply a few sheets of paper rolled up tightly. René Laënnec, a young French doctor, fashioned this first listening device in 1816 in order to examine a young lady. Before Laënnec's invention, doctors simply listened to heart-beats by putting an ear directly on the patient's chest.

Impressed by his new listening device, Laënnec made others of wood in his home *workshop.* He called his listening aid *le cylindre* (the cylinder). Later he changed the name to "stetho-scope," from the Greek *stethos* (chest) and *scope* (I see). Laënnec's stethoscopes were monaural; only one ear at a time was used. Our homemade monaural stethoscope is really simple, but it works great! It probably works a lot better than Dr. Laënnec's original paper stethoscope did!

## WHAT YOU NEED

- one cardboard tube from a paper-towel roll
- aluminum foil
- duct tape

## 1 MAKING IT

1. Place aluminum foil over one end of an empty cardboard tube and fold it tightly down the sides, as shown in **Fig. 1.**
2. Cut the ends of the foil neatly with scissors; this will improve the appearance of your stethoscope.
3. Making sure that the foil is *pulled tightly* over the tube's opening, wrap duct tape over the ends of the foil to hold it taut, as shown in **Fig. 2.**

## 2 USING YOUR STETHOSCOPE

Press the stethoscope's open end against a person's chest about where you think the heart is. Press your ear against the foil end of the stethoscope. You should clearly hear a heartbeat. If you can't, try another place on the person's chest.

Sometimes a doctor will want to hear breathing sounds. Your stethoscope comes in handy here, too! To hear breathing sounds, place the open end of your stethoscope on the person's back, preferably near the center of the upper back. You may hear very little as the person inhales or exhales. This is good, as it means the lungs are clear. Breathing noises may mean the person has a chest cold, or you may hear a wheezing sound if the person has asthma.

The stethoscope can also be used to hear voices and even whispering behind walls or a closed door, or through a window. However, you should never use it to simply listen in on people's private conversations. Being able to overhear secret conversations in a game of international spies or role-playing against alien invaders can be a big plus.

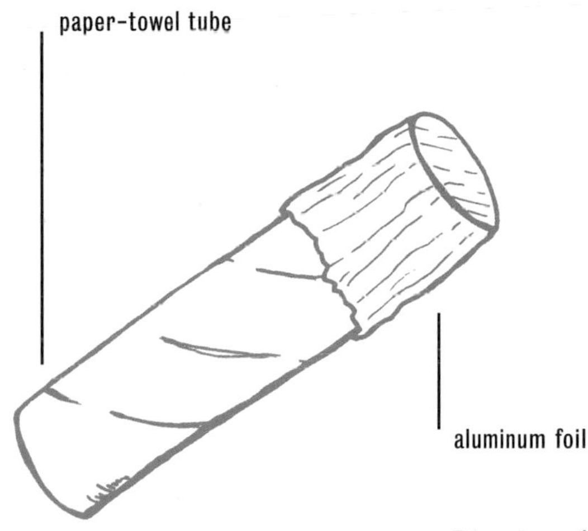


Trim edges of foil with scissors.

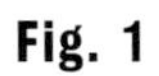

**Fig. 1**

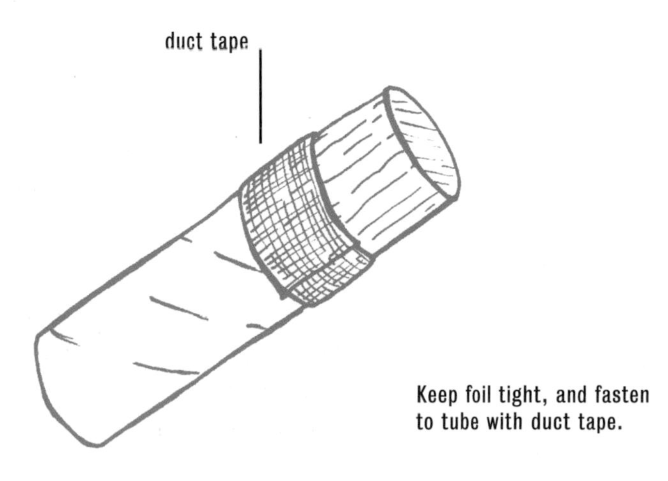


Keep foil tight, and fasten to tube with duct tape.

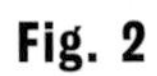

**Fig. 2**

# CONSTELLATION MAKER

Project 4

**Adult Supervision Required**
Use of knife or tool to strip wires.

It may not be as exciting to view a homemade constellation on your bedroom ceiling as it is to look at the real thing outside, but it is more comfortable and will help you recognize constellations when you see them in the night sky.

## WHAT YOU NEED

- one large cylindrical container (such as a 42-ounce oatmeal container)
- aluminum foil
- one rubber band
- one light source (see below)*

* A flashlight can be used for the light source, but it does not make the best type of light for the Constellation Maker. The light from a flashlight spreads out too much. A much better light source is simply a small, bright bulb.

### FOR LIGHT SOURCE:

one 6-volt lantern battery
one PR13 flashlight bulb
2' of stranded electrical wire
duct tape
one slide switch* (optional)

* Simply twist the outside wires together to turn the light on, thus eliminating the switch.

### SEEING STARS

Look up! Did you know that you can see Draco the Dragon on clear nights? No, Draco isn't a fire-breathing dragon. It's a group of stars that seem to form a picture in the sky.

Probably the most familiar group north of the equator is the Big Dipper. It consists of seven stars and is part of the constellation known as Ursa Major, which means Great Bear. The middle star of the handle of the Big Dipper is a double star called Mizar. Look for Mizar the next time you are out on a dark, clear night.

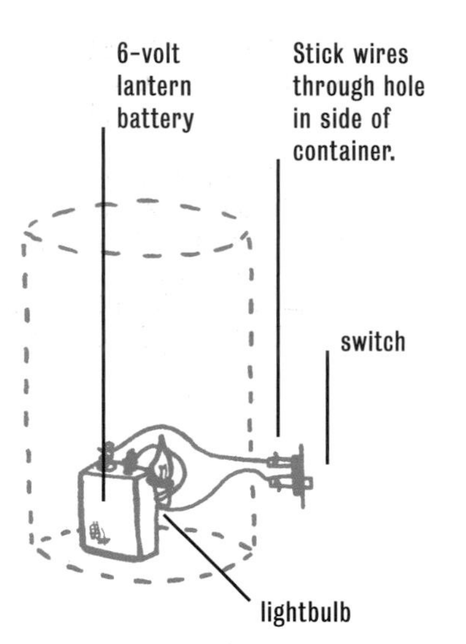


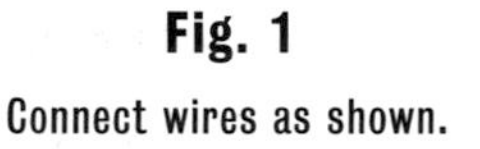
**Fig. 1**

Connect wires as shown.

**Fig. 2**

## 1 MAKING IT

1. Cut a small hole in the side of the cylindrical container, about a third of the way up from the bottom.
2. Strip the insulation from both ends of the electrical wires to expose the bare wire. Twist the bare ends of two of the wires tightly around the battery's spring terminals (see **Fig. 1**). Adding a bit of duct tape to the connection will help keep the wires in good contact with the terminals.
3. Attach the other end of one of the wires connected to a battery terminal to the light bulb, as shown in **Fig. 2.** Attach a third wire to the bottom of the light bulb, as shown in **Fig. 2.** Use a piece of duct tape to tape the bulb's base to the battery. Make sure glass part of bulb is pointing up and not covered with tape.
3. Place the battery and the bulb inside the container. Stick the unattached ends of the wires through the hole in the side of the container (see **Fig. 1**). If desired, attach these loose ends to a switch, as shown in **Fig. 1.**
4. **Fig. 3** is a template that shows the major summer constellations in the United States, Canada, Europe, and Japan as they appear around 10 p.m. local time. Place a photocopy of the template over the aluminum foil. Use a pin or nail to make a tiny hole through the photocopy and into the foil where each star is indicated. Make the hole slightly larger wherever the template shows a brighter star (indicated by a square instead of a circle).
5. As shown in **Fig. 4,** use a rubber band to fasten the aluminum foil over the open end of the container.

## 2 USING IT

At night, place it on a table and turn on the light inside it. The ceiling will turn into a night-sky scene, with the constellations clearly visible. Notice that the template has only the constellations that can be seen all year long in the northern latitudes. These are called circumpolar constellations. Concentrate first on the Big Dipper. Learning to recognize this well-known star pattern will start you off on your quest to uncover the mysteries of the universe.

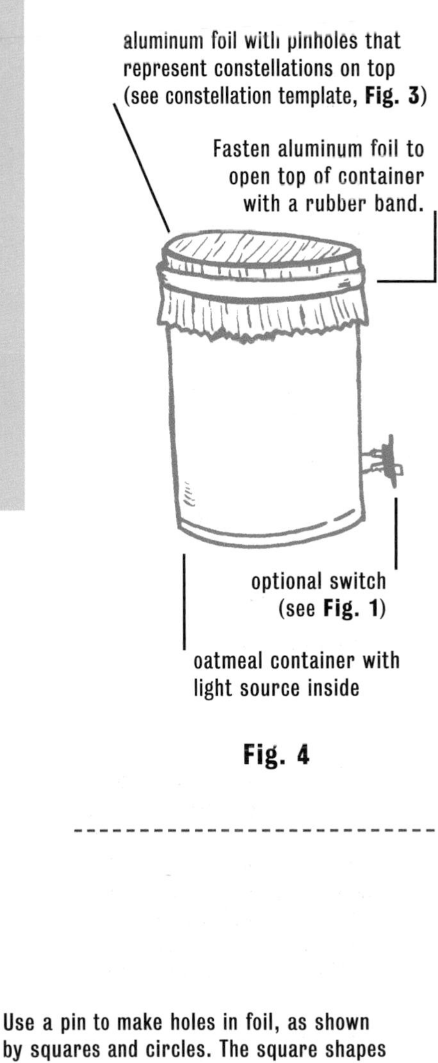


**Fig. 4**

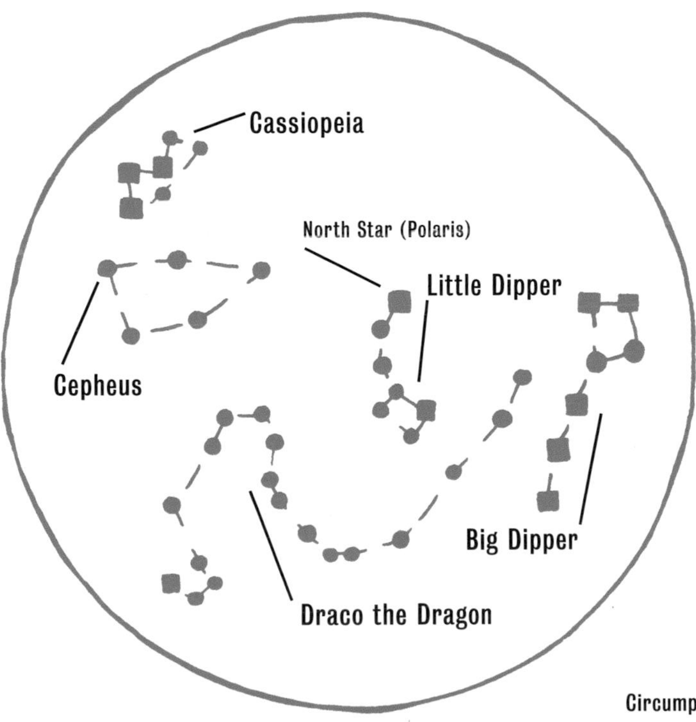


Use a pin to make holes in foil, as shown by squares and circles. The square shapes indicate brighter stars, so make those holes slightly larger than those shown as circles.

**Fig. 3**

Circumpolar Constellations of the Northern Hemisphere

# SEE-SAFE SOLAR VIEWER

Project 5

Looking at the sun directly, even through dark sunglasses, not only is painful but can actually damage your eyes. However, there are simple devices you can make that will let you view the sun's image in complete safety and comfort. All these devices depend on the "pinhole principle" used in the first cameras ever made. The See-Safe Solar Viewer described here is unique because it uses a mirror. This mirror means the size of the viewer can be cut in half.

## WHAT YOU NEED

- one large cylindrical container (such as a 42-ounce oatmeal container)
- one small mirror, to fit inside container
- aluminum foil
- two or three craft sticks
- white paper
- black acrylic craft paint
- craft glue
- epoxy cement

**Fig.** 1 shows the pinhole principle. Notice two things: First, the image of the tree is reversed. Second, the farther you get from the pinhole, the larger the image appears. Although it's not obvious from the drawing, the larger the image, the less bright it is.

## 1 MAKING IT

1. Remove the container's lid and paint the inside of the container black.
2. Using craft glue, glue two layers of white paper to the inside of the lid.
3. As indicated in **Fig.** 2 and **Fig.** 3, cut a 1" hole in the lid and through the white papers.
4. Glue a piece of aluminum foil over the outside of the lid and use a pin to make a tiny hole in the foil as shown in **Fig.** 2.
5. Next, cut a ⅛" peephole in the bottom of the container.
6. As shown in **Fig.** 3, place the small mirror at the bottom of the container. In order to reflect the image so it can be seen through the peephole, the mirror must be raised slightly on the outside end. One way to do this is to glue two or three craft sticks together and then fasten the sticks to the bottom of the container with epoxy cement. Cement the mirror to the craft sticks.

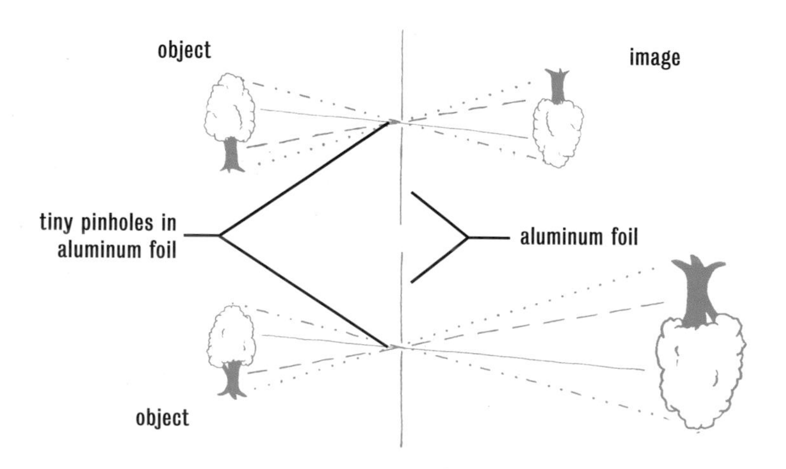

Fig. 1

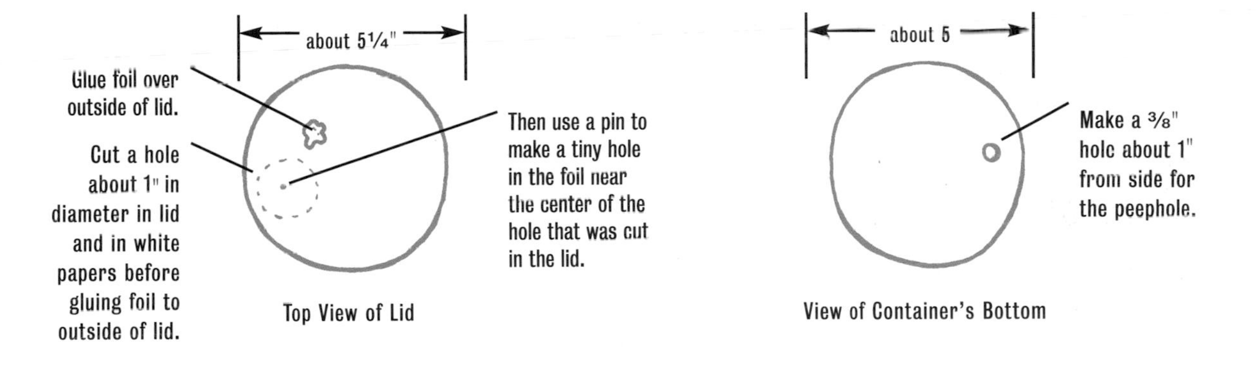
about 5¼"
Glue foil over outside of lid.
Cut a hole about 1" in diameter in lid and in white papers before gluing foil to outside of lid.
Then use a pin to make a tiny hole in the foil near the center of the hole that was cut in the lid.
Top View of Lid
about 5
Make a ⅜" hole about 1" from side for the peephole.
View of Container's Bottom

**Fig. 2**

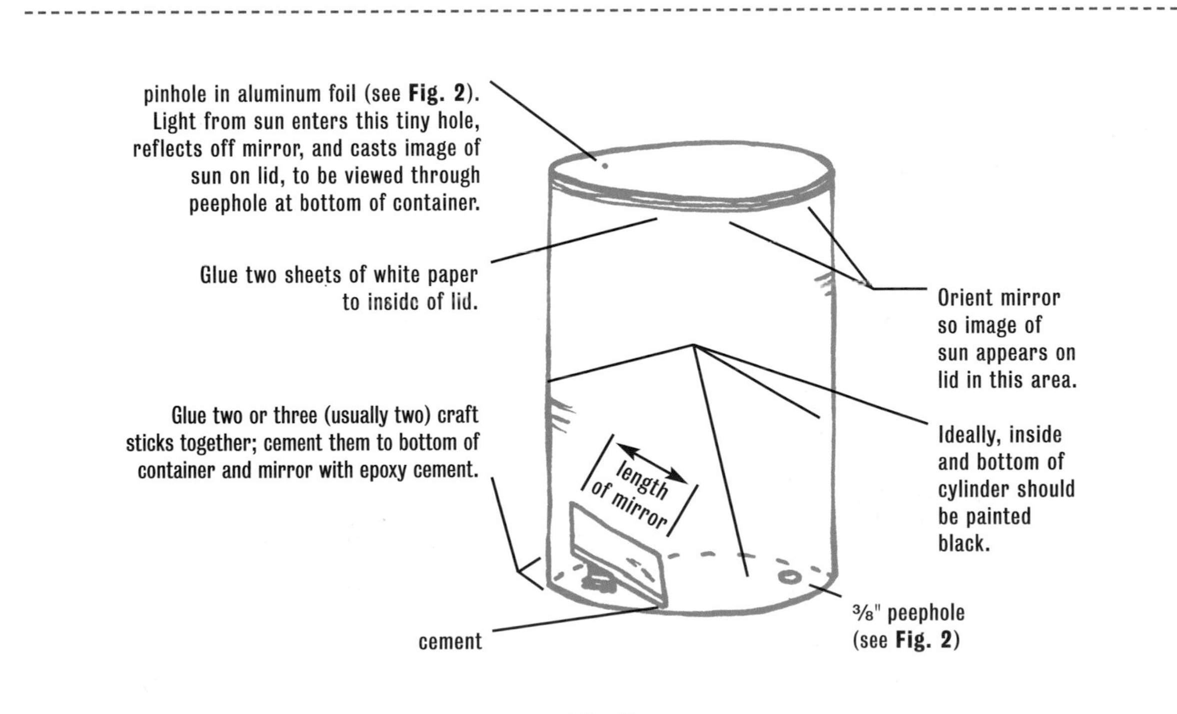
pinhole in aluminum foil (see **Fig. 2**). Light from sun enters this tiny hole, reflects off mirror, and casts image of sun on lid, to be viewed through peephole at bottom of container.
Glue two sheets of white paper to inside of lid.
Orient mirror so image of sun appears on lid in this area.
Glue two or three (usually two) craft sticks together; cement them to bottom of container and mirror with epoxy cement.
length of mirror
Ideally, inside and bottom of cylinder should be painted black.
cement
⅜" peephole (see **Fig. 2**)

**Fig. 3**

## 2 USING IT

The See-Safe Solar Viewer can be used to look at an image of the sun safely during a solar eclipse. There are two solar eclipses each year that can be seen from somewhere on Earth. Check the Internet to see when the next one is due and where it will be visible. Look up "solar eclipse" using one of the search engines.

Although it's most exciting to watch the sun during eclipses, you might see interesting solar phenomena at any time. You may get a chance to observe sunspots, relatively dark "spots" that appear on the sun. While you are watching, you may be lucky enough to see a solar flare. There's no way to predict them, but flares sometimes erupt from the sun's surface and you can see them at the edge of the sun, spewing like a volcano.

As shown in **Fig. 4**, point the solar viewer at the sun and look through the peephole. Move the viewer around until you can see the image of the sun on the inside of the lid. Never look directly at the sun itself. Look at the image of the sun only inside the solar viewer.

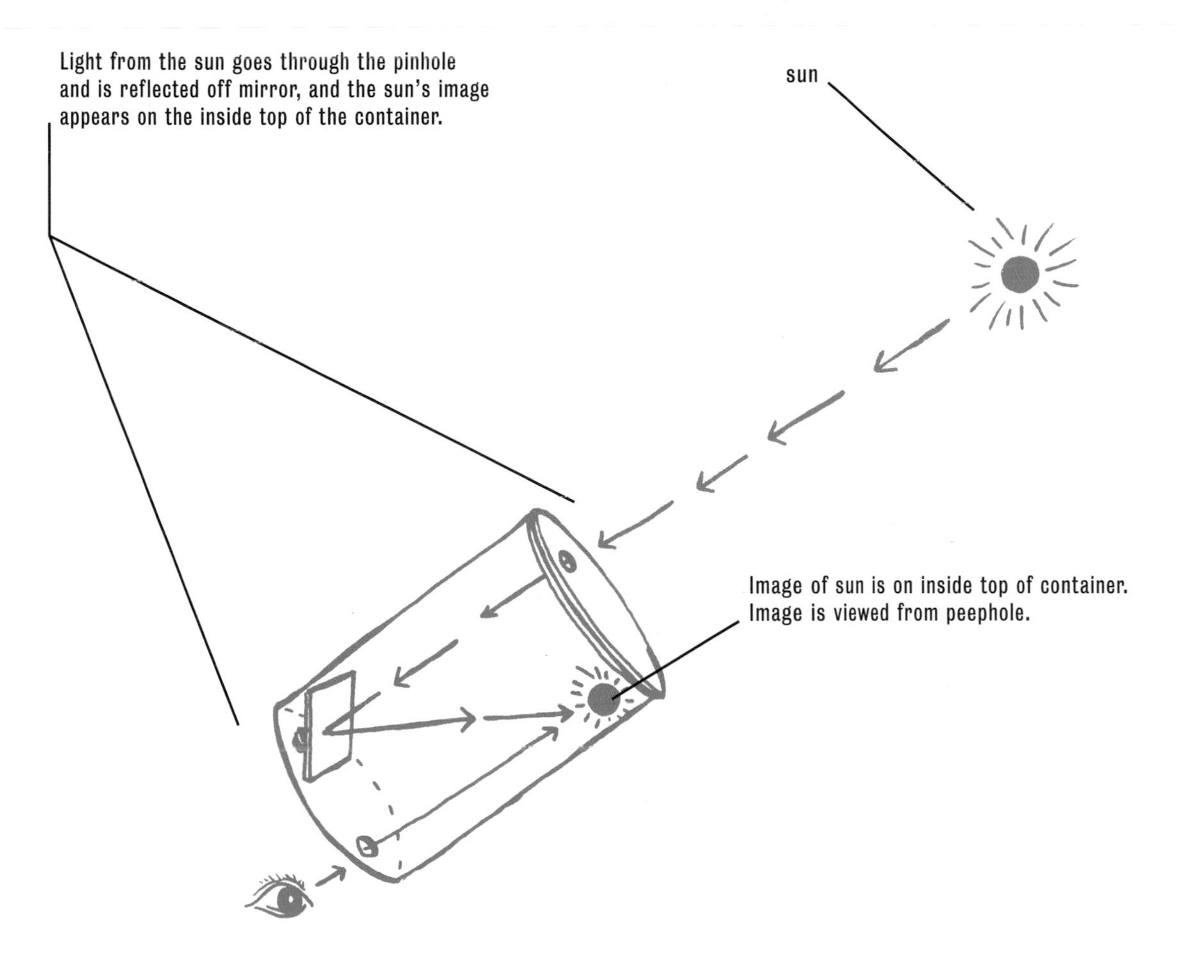


WARNING: NEVER LOOK AT SUN DIRECTLY. ONLY LOOK AT ITS IMAGE IN VIEWER.

**Fig. 4**

# AUTOMATIC CAT/DOG FEEDER

Project 6

**Adult Supervision Required**
Use of drill or sharp object for holes.

Kids aren't the only ones who love food-related gadgets—pets, especially cats, love them, too! Here I will show you how to make a snack dispenser for your cat or small dog. What makes it even more fun is that you can construct it almost entirely out of stuff your mom and dad normally throw out!

## WHAT YOU NEED

- one large cylindrical container (such as a 42-ounce oatmeal container) with lid
- one small rubber or plastic ball
- one small cardboard box (about 7" wide, 6" deep, and 10" long)
- several inches of string
- one large, heavyweight rubber band
- 2" × 3" piece of cardboard or plastic container lid
- one craft stick
- glue (white, wood, or craft)
- duct tape
- cardboard for chute (optional)
- heavyweight paper for funnel (optional)

### WHAT THE AUTOMATIC CAT/DOG FEEDER DOES

Cat or dog food is put in the container on top. Every time the pet paws at the rubber or plastic ball, food drops through a trapdoor and slides down a chute so the pet can reach it. It may take a bit of training to show the pet what to do to get a snack, but once the pet learns the drill, it will be able to feed itself!

## 1 MAKING IT

It's possible to construct the Automatic Cat/Dog Feeder simply by following **Fig. 1**. If you have questions, look at **Figs. 2, 3,** and **4**.

1. Start by cutting a 1½" square hole in the middle of the bottom of the container.
2. Next, tape a 2" × 3" piece of cardboard, or a plastic lid, to the bottom as shown in **Fig. 1** and **Fig. 2**. This is the trapdoor. Make a small hole about ⅛" diameter in the trapdoor as indicated in **Fig. 2**.
3. Make a small hole in the center of the container's lid. Tie one end of a rubber strip (from a large rubber band) to a craft stick. String the other end of the rubber strip through the hole in the container's lid. Pull the rubber strip down, string it through the hole in the trapdoor, and tie its end to a 1" length of a small craft stick as shown in **Fig. 1** and **Fig. 2**. Make sure the rubber is taut enough so it keeps the trapdoor shut tight.
4. Open a small cardboard box and lay it upside down so it sits on its opened flaps. Cut a hole about 3" square in the box's bottom and set the container over this hole. Glue the container to the box.
5. As shown in **Fig. 1**, make a small hole in one side of the box and pass a string through this hole. Put the end of the string through the same hole where you strung the rubber strip and tie it to the rubber strip as shown in **Fig. 1** and **Fig. 2**. So your pet can get to the food, cut and remove a large section of one side of the box, or simply cut one side out completely.
6. Use a drill or sharp object to make a hole through the ball and pull the end of the string through this hole. Tie the end of the string so that the ball is pushed up against the side of the box.
7. In order to make sure all the food can get out of the container, you may want to use a piece of heavyweight paper to make a funnel in the container. Look again at **Fig. 1**. If your pet has trouble getting to food that has dropped through the trapdoor, try adding a cardboard chute directly under the trapdoor—the chute design that works with your pet is left to your ingenuity.
8. Now all you have to do is fill the container with cat or dog food, do a few test runs, and then show your pet how much fun it is to use the Automatic Cat/Dog Feeder!

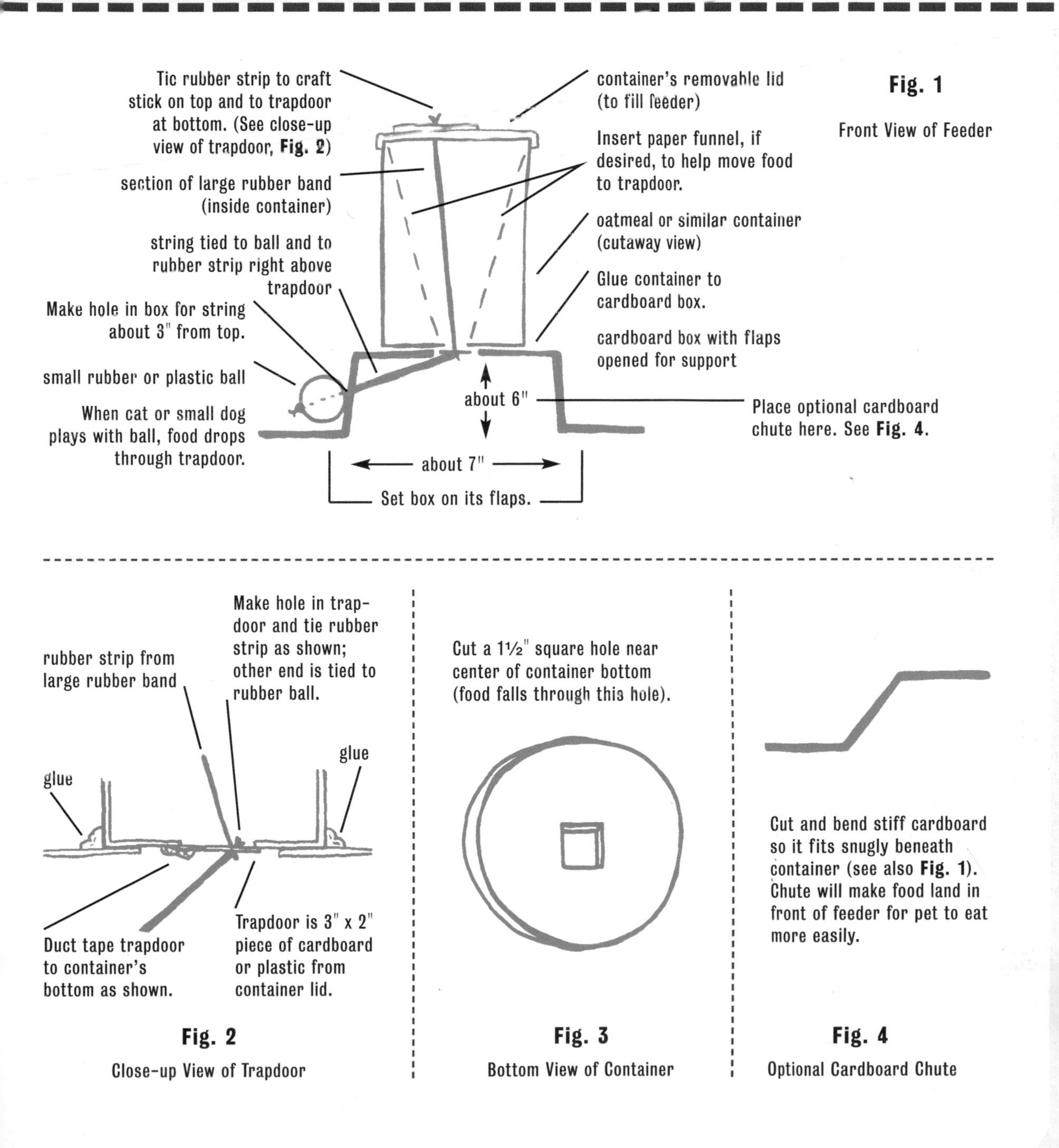


**Fig. 1**

Front View of Feeder



**Fig. 2**

Close-up View of Trapdoor



**Fig. 3**

Bottom View of Container



**Fig. 4**

Optional Cardboard Chute

# AUTO-FILL WATER DISH

Project 7

**Adult Supervision Required**
**Use of drill, tin snips, file. Sharp edges.**

Give yourself and your cat, dog, or other pet a break by building an amazing automatic watering hole! This water boy, which never gets tired or bored, makes taking care of a pet easier—plus, it's fun to watch it work! It keeps your pet's water dish filled with clean water automatically—and will never overfill it and make a mess! How does it work? The construction is simple, but the theory behind it is a bit harder to understand. Its operation uses the principle of air pressure and partial vacuum (see page 38). This complex operation, even if construction is easy, is one reason I love to watch this amazing Auto-Fill Water Dish work!

## WHAT YOU NEED

- two 2-liter plastic soda bottles
- one 2- to 3-pound coffee can with plastic lid (remove label and paint the can, if desired)
- one plastic pet dish
- 2" length of plastic tubing (5/16" inside diameter)
- one 1" 6-32 machine screw
- one 6-32 machine screw nut
- small washer
- 6" length of picture-hanger wire
- duct tape
- contact cement
- epoxy cement
- one funnel (optional; makes filling soda bottle easier)
- one empty gallon milk jug to store water (optional)
- sand or small stones to weigh down can (optional)

# 1 MAKING IT

1. As shown in **Fig.** 1, drill a 1/16" hole in the exact center of the bottom of one of the soda bottles. Also, make a 7/16" hole near the top, as shown.
2. Cut the water trough from a second plastic 2-liter soda bottle, using **Fig.** 2 as a guide. Scissors can be used to make the cuts, but it is easier if tin snips are used to cut the soda bottle's bottom. Discard unused portions of this bottle.
3. Use tin snips to cut out a notch near the coffee can's top (see **Fig.** 3). Also, directly opposite this notch, drill a 5/16" hole about ¾" from the can's top.
4. Make a ½" hole directly in the middle of the coffee can's plastic top. See **Fig.** 4.

# 2 ASSEMBLING THE PARTS

1. **Fig.** 5 gives details on putting the Auto-Fill Water Dish together. To make the pet watering hole more stable, put some sand or stones at the bottom of the coffee can to add weight.
2. Use a nail or a drill to make a hole about ⅛" in diameter in the back of the trough. Next, mount the plastic water trough to the inside of the coffee can with a 1" 6-32 machine screw, nut, and washer, using the hole you just made for the screw.
3. Use contact cement to glue the bottom of the soda bottle to the lid of the coffee can, making sure the hole in the bottom of the soda bottle and the hole in the lid are aligned. Be sure to follow the manufacturer's instructions for the contact cement.
4. Insert one end of the tube in the 5/16" hole you made in the bottle. Use epoxy cement to seal the space between the tube and the bottle. Use duct tape to fasten the tube to the bottle (see **Fig.** 5).
5. Drill two small holes in the side of the plastic dish. Place the other end of the tube in the water dish. This end of the tube is used to sense the depth of the water.
6. As shown in **Fig.** 5, thread wire through the holes in the plastic dish and around the tube to attach the tube to the dish. (You will probably want to shorten the tube to make the dish sit better.)

# 3 ADJUSTING THE WATER LEVEL

To add water to the Auto-Fill Water Dish, remove the cap from the soda bottle and pour water into the bottle. A funnel comes in handy for this step, but it isn't essential. Make sure you put the cap back on the bottle tightly, since the bottle must be sealed for the Auto-Fill Water Dish to work right. You can set the depth of the water in the dish by adjusting where the end of the tube is. If you want 2" of water in the dish, put the end of the tube 2" from the bottom of the dish. If you want more water, raise the end of the tube a bit.

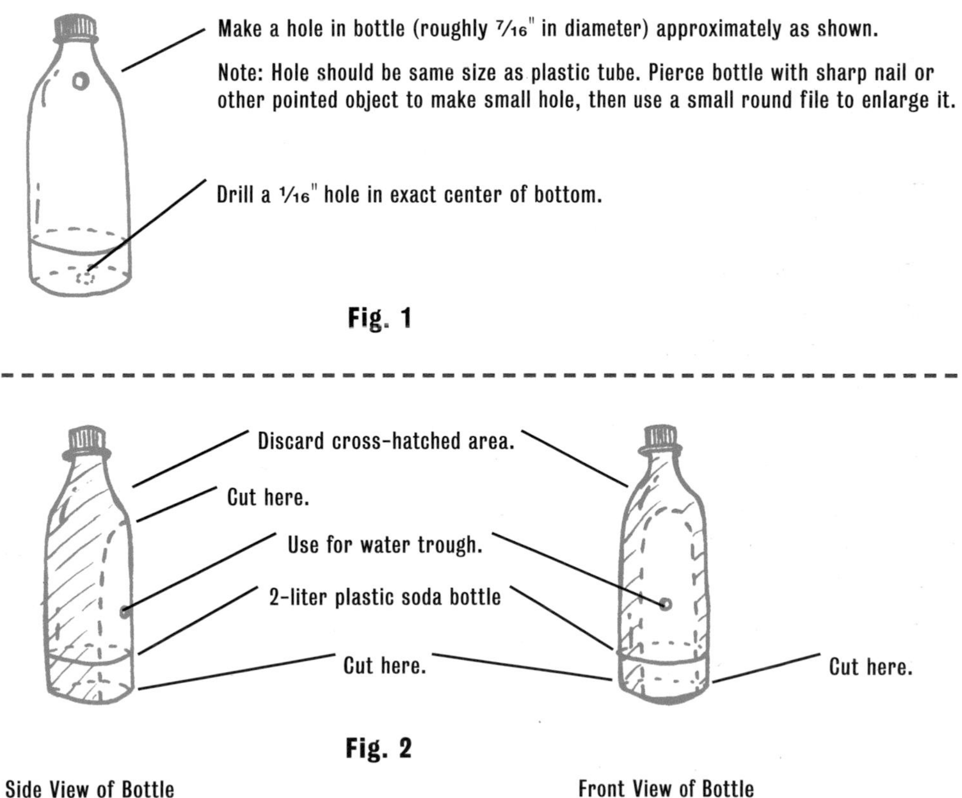


Fig. 1

Fig. 2

## AIR PRESSURE AND PARTIAL VACUUM

Everywhere on Earth, there's roughly 14 pounds of force pushing against every square inch...on everything! Where does this force come from? From air pressure. If it weren't for air pressure, we would all suffocate! If the force pushing against each square inch in a container is substantially below this, say only 12 pounds or less, we say there is a "partial vacuum" in the container. A simple way to make a "partial vacuum" is to put a tiny hole in the cap of a soda bottle. Half fill the bottle with water. Place the cap on it. Then turn the bottle upside down. You'll notice that some water comes out of the bottle's cap. The top of the bottle, which doesn't have any water, is now under a "partial vacuum." Notice something now. Even though the bottle is upside down and there is a hole in the cap, no more water comes out! That's because there is just as much force pushing UP as pushing DOWN. The reason why the pressure of the air above the water MUST be lower than the outside air pressure in order for the water to stop coming through the hole is that WATER HAS WEIGHT! The difference in pressure between the partial vacuum in the top of the bottle and the outside air must be enough to counterbalance the weight of the water! By the way, if you were on the moon what would the water in the bottle do? All come out? None of the water come out? The same as if it was on Earth? Also, what would the water do if the bottle was orbiting earth inside the Space Shuttle? I know the answer, do you?

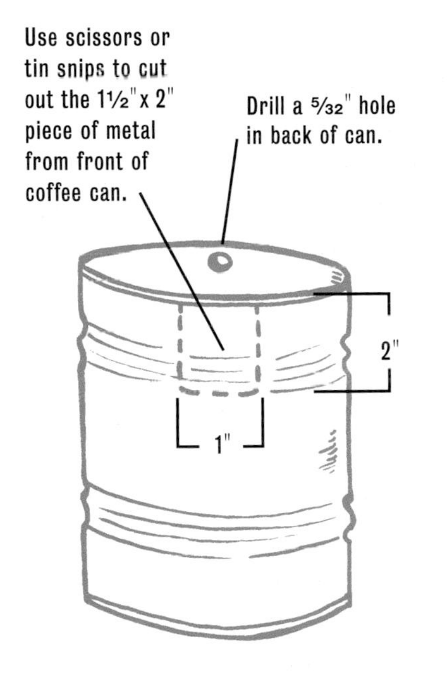


**Fig. 3**

Front View of Coffee Can

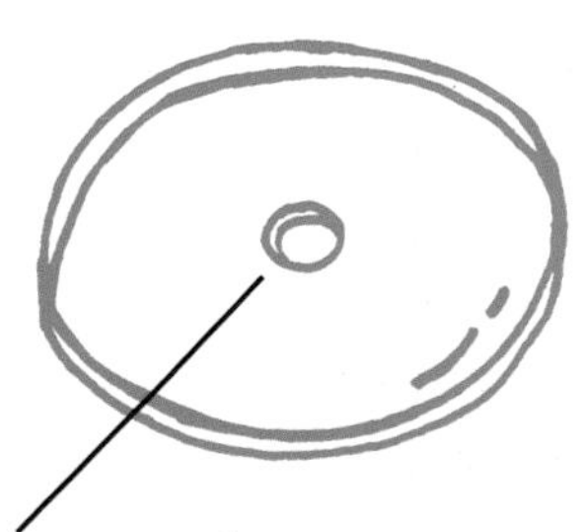

Make a ½" hole in the center of the coffee can's plastic lid.

**Fig. 4**

Top View of Coffee Can's Plastic Lid

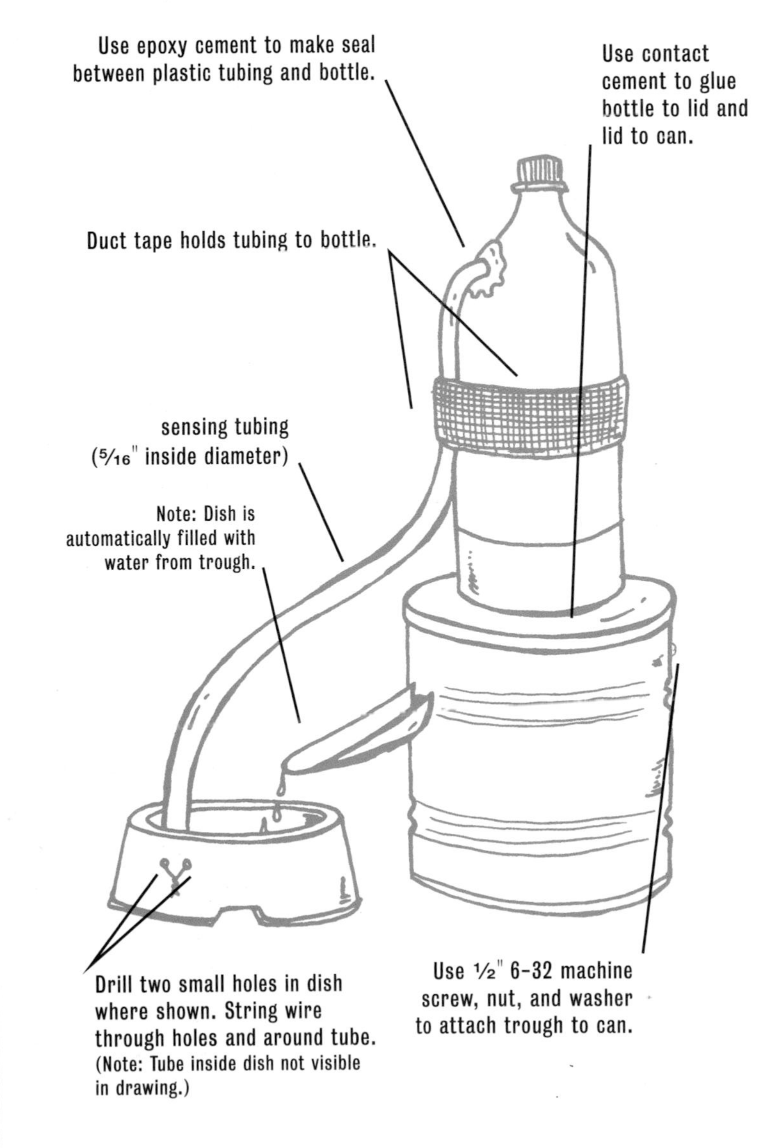

**Fig. 5**

# GIANT-PUMPKIN GROWER

Project 8

**Adult Supervision Required**
**Use of tools, staple gun.**

Before you start your Giant-Pumpkin Grower, I have to warn you—huge pumpkins have huge trailing vines. The area needed to plant your pumpkins can be small, but the vines will want to spread out. So you'd better ask your parents if it's okay to have pumpkin vines crawling all over the lawn.

The easiest way to grow pumpkins this size is to start the seeds in a pumpkin "house." The plastic-covered wooden frame protects the seeds and tiny plants from the cold, hot winds, bugs, and many animals who love to eat the seeds. The same Giant-Pumpkin Grower can also speed up growth after young plants are placed in the garden. Rapid early growth often increases the size of the vine. Remember, giant pumpkins need giant vines!

## WHAT YOU NEED

- six 1 × 2 boards, 31" long
- two 1 × 2 boards, 48" long
- one 1 × 2 board, 46½" long
- nine wood screws (2" long #8) or eighteen small nails (4d)
- three 6-32 machine screws, 2" long
- three 6-32 nuts
- staples or tacks
- clear plastic sheeting – 3 mil weight or more, available at hardware and home improvement stores

**FOR PLANTING:**

- potting soil
- large peat pots

# 1 MAKING IT

The Giant-Pumpkin Grower is made from 1 × 2 lumber and clear plastic sheeting.

1. To make each side, attach the boards as shown in **Fig. 1** with either wood screws or nails, using **Figs.** 1, 2, and 3 as a guide. The short boards are screwed or nailed to the long boards so they are perpendicular to them. First only attach the short boards to the long boards with one screw or nail. When you are sure the short boards are parallel with each other and perpendicular to the long boards use the second screw or nail at each end to make the sides stiff. A helper here comes in handy.
2. As shown in **Fig.** 2, round one end of the three boards of side B approximately ½" from the corners using a wood file. This will allow you to fold up the Giant-Pumpkin Grower until its next use.
3. Drill the 5⁄32" hole after side A and side B are made so the holes will align.
4. After loosely bolting the frames together (remember side B is attached to the inside of side A), fold side A and side B together.
5. Staple or tack clear plastic film to both sides but not to the ends. Open up the frame to the desired position and staple triangular-shaped pieces of plastic to both ends.

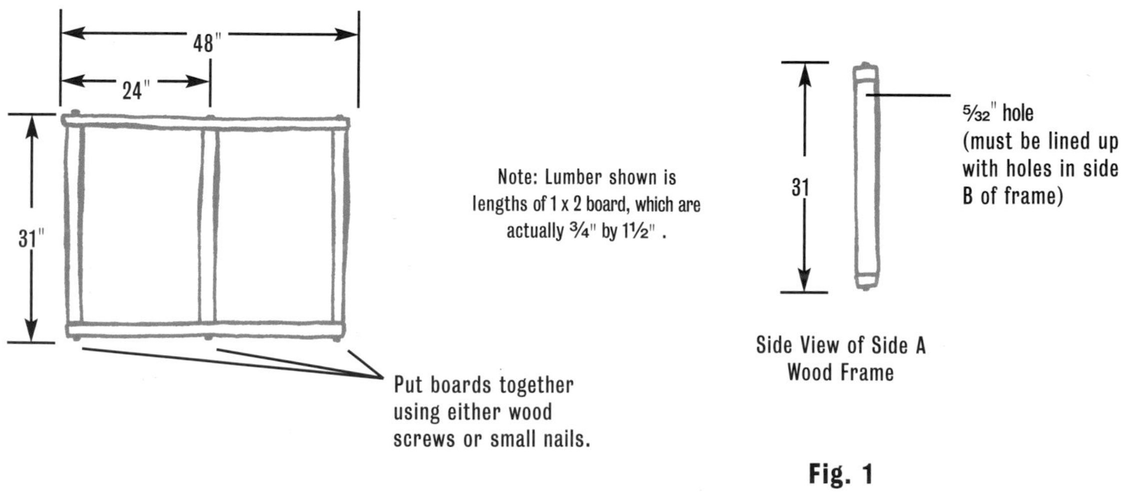


**Fig. 1**

Construction of Side A

# 2 PLANTING THE SEEDS

Three varieties of pumpkin reliably produce giant pumpkins: Atlantic Giant, Prizewinner, and Big Moon. Prizewinner produces the best-looking pumpkins. Atlantic Giant is supposed to produce the largest ones.

You will need potting soil and large peat pots. Make sure you use only good, light potting soil—not the heavy, dark, cheap stuff. If you live in a central U.S. latitude (the Denver, Chicago, Cleveland, and New York areas), plant the seeds in the pots around May 1. Farther north, plant a little later (up to a month later along the Canadian border); farther south, a little earlier (over a month earlier in the deep South).

1. Fill the peat pots to within ½" of the top with damp potting soil. Pack down the soil gently.
2. Place two or three seeds, evenly spaced, 1" deep in each pot.
3. Water well and put the pots outside in a sunny place. Set the Giant-Pumpkin Grower over them. With sunny weather, and if you water lightly every third day, you should see the first leaves poking up in about ten days.

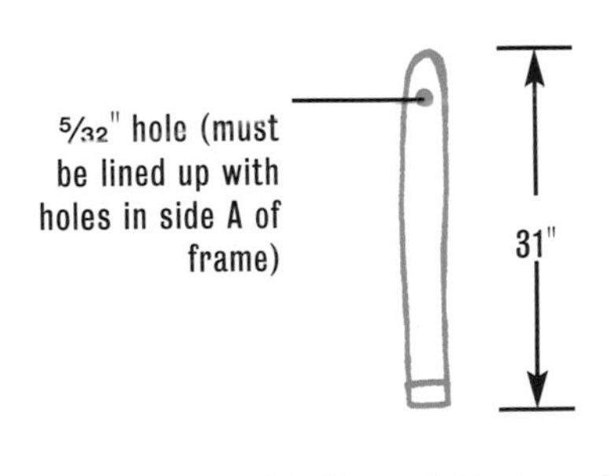


Side View of Side B Wood Frame

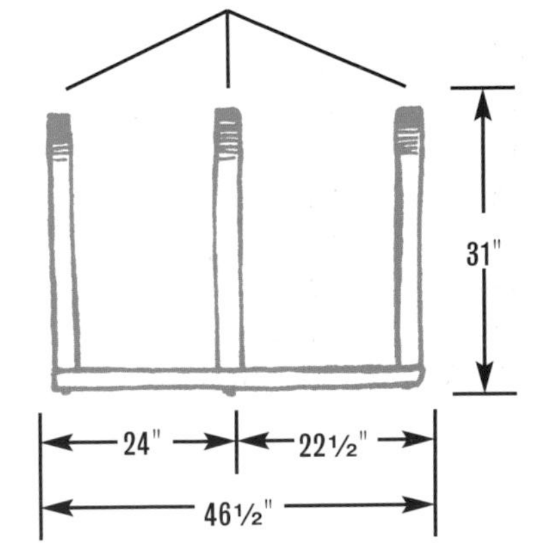


Front View of Side B

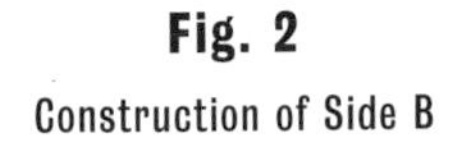

**Fig. 2**
Construction of Side B

When the pumpkin plants have sprouted, plant them in the garden. Before planting, read the section on Gardening Tips (at right). When planting, put the whole peat pot in the ground, but leave the pumpkin's leaves free above the ground. Water well and place the Giant-Pumpkin Grower over the plants. To weigh the Giant-Pumpkin Grower down, fill two used milk jugs with water. Using a short length of rope, tie a jug to each end and place the rope over the Giant-Pumpkin Grower.

Every few days take the Giant-Pumpkin Grower off the plants temporarily and water them. Once the pumpkin's vines fill the grower, remove it. For the biggest pumpkins, sprinkle a little fertilizer on the ground near the pumpkins. Don't get any on the leaves! If you do you will damage them. Apply water. Pick bugs off the leaves every day during the first two weeks after removing the Giant-Pumpkin Grower.

## 3 HARVESTING

For the best and largest pumpkins, pick them in early October or shortly before the first frost. If you save the seeds from your biggest pumpkin, not only will you save money, but next year maybe you'll grow an even bigger pumpkin!

The two sides of the Giant-Pumpkin Grower frame are attached with three 2" 6-32 screws and nuts. Finger-tighten only!

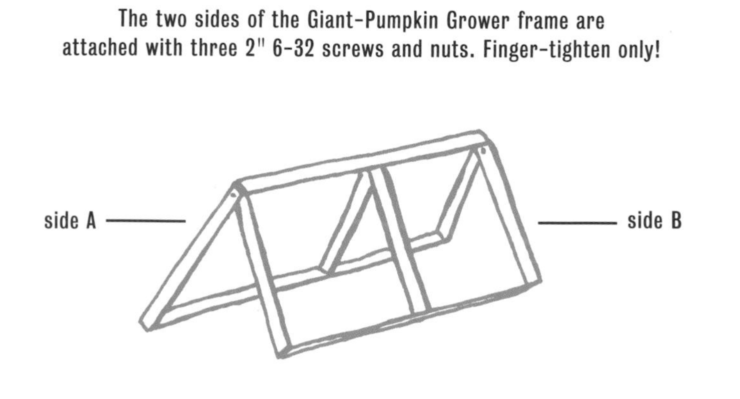


**Fig. 3**
Attaching Side A and Side B of Wood Frame

**SEEDS VERSUS PLANTS TIP**

**It's easiest to grow tomatoes, peppers, and most flowers by buying plants. Most vegetables, however, other than those mentioned, are best grown from seeds.**

# 4 GARDENING TIPS

Plants need soil, water, and sunshine. All vegetables and most flowers grow best in a sunny spot. If you want to grow vegetables, fertilize the soil before you plant. Sprinkle about one pound (about two cups) of a general-purpose fertilizer (such as 12-12-12 or 5-10-5) or five pounds of dried cow manure for every 100 square feet of garden space (100 square feet is about the size of a small room). For example, if your garden is 20' by 10' (20 multiplied by 10 = 200 square feet) you would sprinkle about two pounds of fertilizer or ten pounds of dried cow manure on it. For really great growth and lots of good things to eat, you will need to double the amount of fertilizer. But beware! Don't use too much fertilizer! You can actually kill your plants if you use too much fertilizer. And if you are growing flowers, use less fertilizer.

The least expensive way to purchase fertilizer is in fifty-pound bags, which are available at garden centers and many hardware stores. This much fertilizer may last you several years—if your parents don't use it on the lawn, that is!

After spreading the fertilizer, mix it into the soil with a shovel or garden hoe. Don't leave soil lumps larger than a golf ball. Once this is done, the soil is prepared for planting.

## WHEN TO PLANT

The best time to plant depends on where you live and what you want to plant. Many vegetables, and some flowers, are best planted very early—about the time daffodils bloom. These "cool-weather" vegetables include peas, lettuce, radishes, and carrots. "Warm-weather" vegetables should be planted only when the weather is warm. When the oak leaves are a couple of inches long or when you start seeing tomato and flower plants being sold outside in farmer's markets and roadside stands, it is usually safe to plant warm-weather vegetables. Warm-weather vegetables include corn, tomatoes, cucumbers, melons, and pumpkins.

If there isn't at least one good rain every week, water the garden well that week. Hoe and pull out all weeds. It's easiest and best to hoe and pull weeds while they are still small. This usually means that you should weed your garden at least once a week.

# SNOWBALL LAUNCHER

Project 9

**Adult Supervision Required**
**Use of tools, drill. Sharp edges.**

**A good throwing arm is handy for snowball fights. But your arm can get tired, especially during long-distance battles, which are really the most fun. When opponents are quite a distance apart, you rarely get a snowball in your face or down your back. (You seldom even get hit!) Despite this, the thrill is there. The Snowball Launcher described here is perfect for snowball fights when the distance is more than 20 feet. And for a well-equipped snow fort, it's the ideal "heavy artillery."**

## WHAT YOU NEED

- two 2 × 4 boards, 12" long
- one 2 × 4 board, 36" long
- one 2 × 4 board, 72" long
- one small board (4" piece of a 1 × 2 or similar)
- one small piece of wood (to place inside can and hold eye hook)
- two 5/16" machine bolts, 4" long, with nuts
- two 8-32 machine screws, 2" long, with nuts and washers
- four #10 wood screws, 3" long
- one short but wide can
- one screen-door hook (with screw-in attachment) – this is the "launcher's" trigger
- two 1"-long 6-32 machine screws with nuts and washers
- one eye hook (with wood threads)
- three small nails (6d)
- four (preferably more) heavy-duty rubber bands, 5" long and 5/8" wide (cut to 10"-long strips)*
- snow (an absolute necessity!)

*These rubber strips should be stretched several times before use or they won't last long.

# 1 MAKING IT

1. Cut all boards to the lengths indicated.
2. Make sure there are no sharp edges in or on the can. If there are, use a file to smooth them. Drill two ⅛" holes in the sides of the can around 1" from top and opposite each other. These holes are for the machine screws, which are used to attach the rubber strips. Also, drill ¼" hole in the center of the bottom of the can for the eye hook, using **Fig. 1** as a guide. To attach the eye hook to the bottom of the can, first place a small piece of wood inside the can, then screw the eye hook into it.
3. Drill a 3⁄16" hole about 2" from one end of each of the 12" boards. These are the upper arms of the Snowball Launcher. Insert 8-32 screws in the upper arms. Rubber strips are attached to the ends of these screws. See the instructions given for attaching these, in the box at right.
4. The 3' crossbar is attached to the 6' center bar about 6" from the center launching board's end. To do this, you will need help centering the crossbar over the center launching board and drilling a 5⁄6" hole directly through both boards. Next, use two 5⁄16" bolts and nuts to attach the 2 boards together.

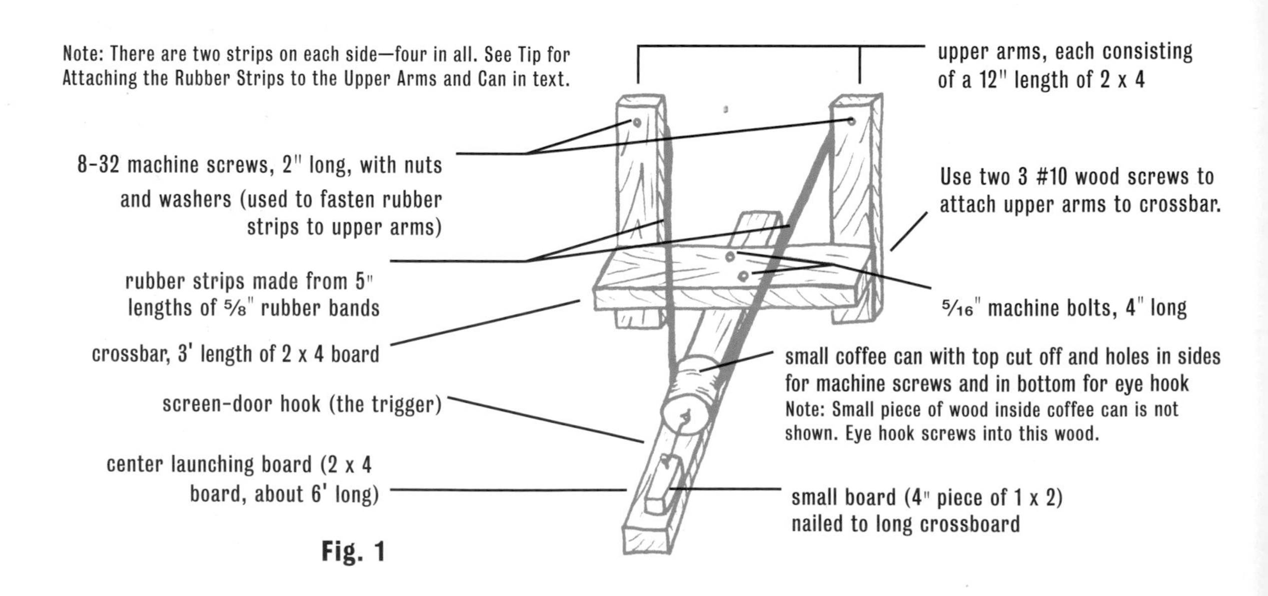


Fig. 1

5. Using **Fig.** 1 as a guide, use two 3"-long #10 wood screws to attach each upper arm to the ends of the crossbar. (Note: 16d nails can be used to do this instead of wood screws.)
6. Attach the rubber strips, made from rubber bands, to the can using 6-32 machine screws and nuts. (See attachment instructions in the box at right.) Make sure these screws are very tight! Altogether, four rubber bands are used in the Snowball Launcher. Each set of rubber bands should last for about twenty-five throws. Make sure you always have plenty of spare rubber bands handy!
7. Attach the screen door's eye hook to a small 1 × 4 piece of wood, about ½" from an end. Push eye hook through hole in bottom of can. Attach the "trigger" to the can's eyehook and then pull on the can and block until it is hard to pull anymore. Then use three 6d nails to fasten the board to the center launching board.

## 2 TRYING IT OUT

You can support the Snowball Launcher on a sawhorse, or you can place it on top of a snow fort or a big mound of firm snow. Actually, snow makes the best support because the height can be easily adjusted.

Next, make a good-sized snowball and place it in the can. Use different sizes for different distances—smaller snowballs go farther. Pull back the can and use the screen-door hook to hold the can in place while you wait to launch. When you are ready, use your finger to push the hook down (or up) to release the can. Then watch the ball sail through the air, hopefully striking its target!

*Caution: Use the Snowball Launcher to throw soft, freshly made snowballs only. Don't throw rocks or ice!*

**TIP FOR ATTACHING THE RUBBER STRIPS TO THE UPPER ARMS AND CAN**

First make a tiny hole, using a small nail or large pin, near the ends of all the rubber strips. To attach the rubber strips to the can, pass a machine screw through the hole in the can (from the inside out) and put a washer on the end of it. Then attach the first rubber strip (push the tiny hole in the rubber strip over the end of the screw) and add a second washer. Next, push the hole of the second rubber strip over the screw and add a final washer and then a nut. See Fig. 2.

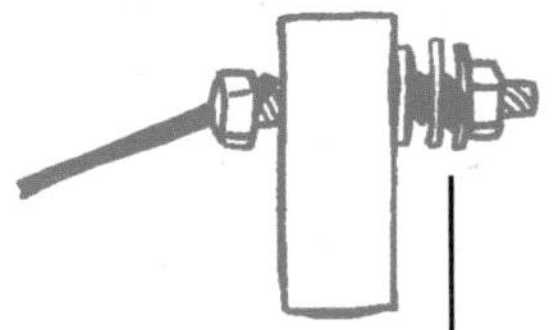

Place rubber strips between washers onto screw.

**Fig. 2**

# SUPER-DUPER WATER SHOOTER

Project 10

**Adult Supervision Required**
Use of drill and tools.

"Fantastic!" "Awesome!" "Formidable!" These are some of the words my oldest son, Mark, used when he first saw the Super-Duper Water Shooter in operation. If Mark had made the water shooter, he probably would have added the phrase "easy to make" to his description.

## WHAT YOU NEED

- one 2' length of ½"-inside-diameter CPVC rigid plastic water pipe (body)
- one 2' length of a ⅜"-diameter wood dowel (plunger)
- one 2" length of a ½"-diameter wood dowel (nozzle)
- one ½" (00) faucet washer
- one 1" #6 wood screw
- petroleum jelly
- one empty plastic gallon milk jug to hold water (optional)
- one 3" length of a ¾" wood dowel for handle (optional)
- wood glue for handle (optional)
- electrical or narrow duct tape for more secure grip (optional)

## 1 MAKING IT

1. To make the nozzle, use a 1/16" drill bit to make a hole in the center of a 2" length of a ½"-diameter wood dowel. Next, use a small hammer to tap this nozzle into the end of the ½" pipe. If the nozzle seems a bit too large to fit, sand it and try again. While the nozzle should be snug in the pipe, don't hammer it in so hard that you break the pipe! See **Fig.** 1.
2. Using a 7/64" drill bit, drill a pilot hole in the center of one end of the ⅜" wood dowel.
3. Next, attach the faucet washer to the dowel end with the #6 wood screw. Don't over tighten the screw. This wood dowel and washer combination is the "shooter's" plunger. See **Fig.** 2.
4. Using **Figs.** 3 and 4 as a guide, stick the plunger in the pipe. It should fit somewhat snugly but still be easy to move. If it sticks in the pipe, gently sand the washer using fine sandpaper until you can stick the plunger into the pipe without pushing very hard.
5. Next, place a bit of petroleum jelly on the washer.

If you want, the shooter can be used as is. Nonetheless, you may want to add two more "improvements."

## 2 SPECIAL ADD-ONS

You may want to add tape to the body to make the shooter easier to grip, as shown in **Fig.** 6. Also, you can attach a handle to the plunger. To do this, use a ⅜" bit to drill a hole about halfway through a 3" length of a ¾"-diameter wood dowel (see **Figs.** 5 and 6).

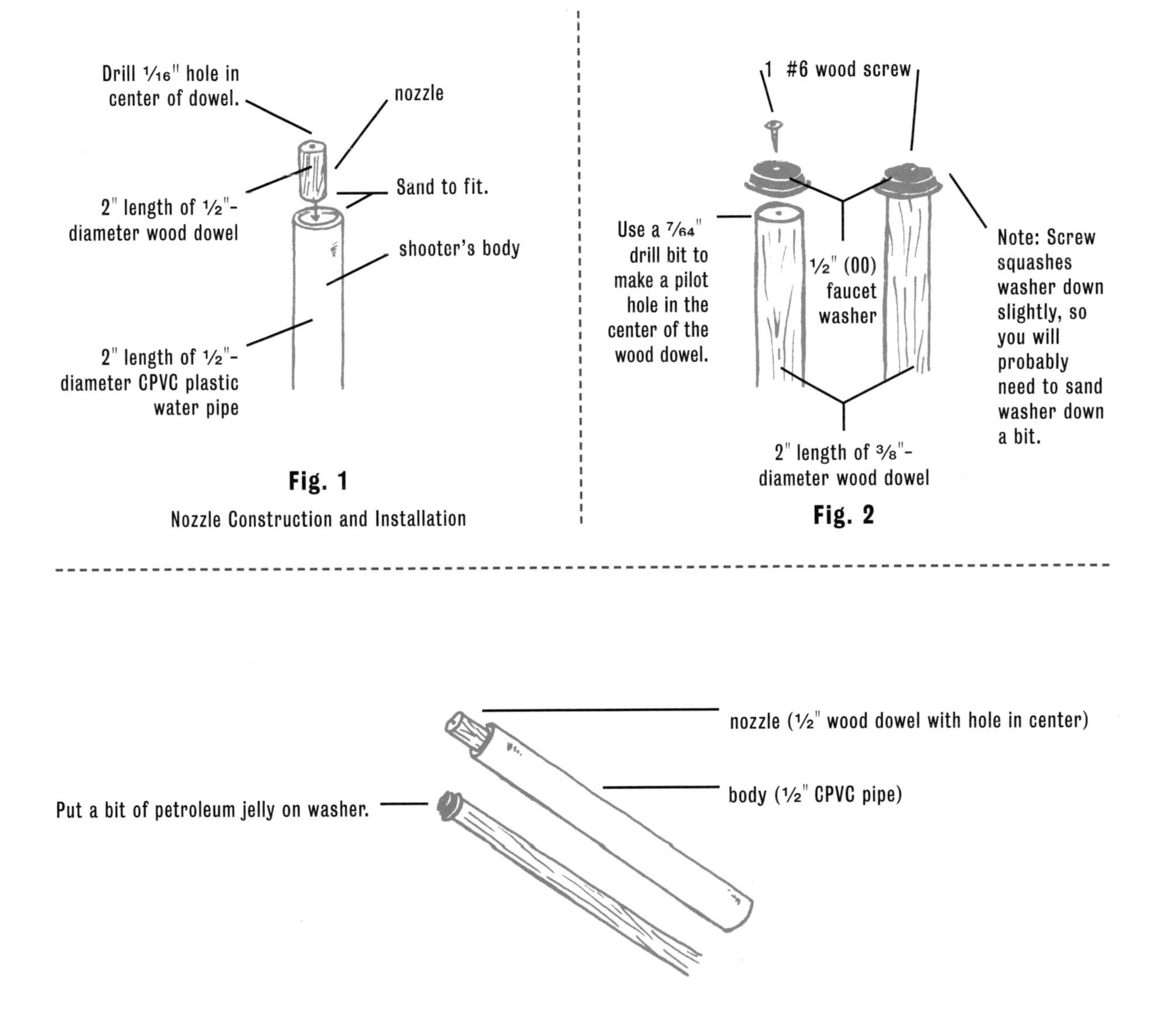
Drill 1/16" hole in center of dowel.
nozzle
Sand to fit.
2" length of 1/2"-diameter wood dowel
shooter's body
2" length of 1/2"-diameter CPVC plastic water pipe
Fig. 1
Nozzle Construction and Installation
1 #6 wood screw
Use a 7/64" drill bit to make a pilot hole in the center of the wood dowel.
1/2" (00) faucet washer
Note: Screw squashes washer down slightly, so you will probably need to sand washer down a bit.
2" length of 3/8"-diameter wood dowel
Fig. 2
nozzle (1/2" wood dowel with hole in center)
body (1/2" CPVC pipe)
Put a bit of petroleum jelly on washer.

**Fig. 3**

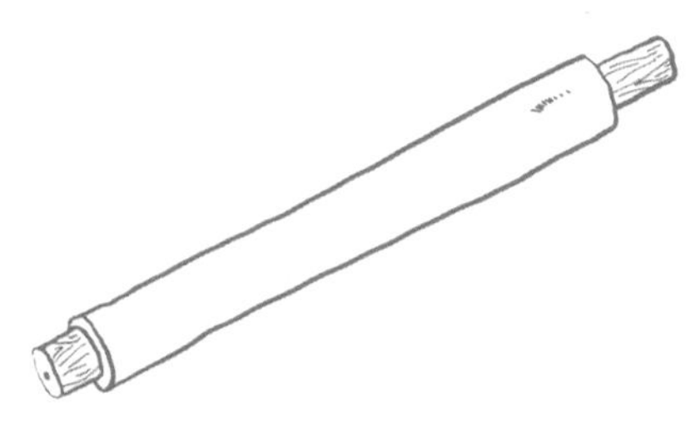

**Fig. 4**

The "basic" Super-Duper Water Shooter consists of three components: nozzle, body, and plunger.

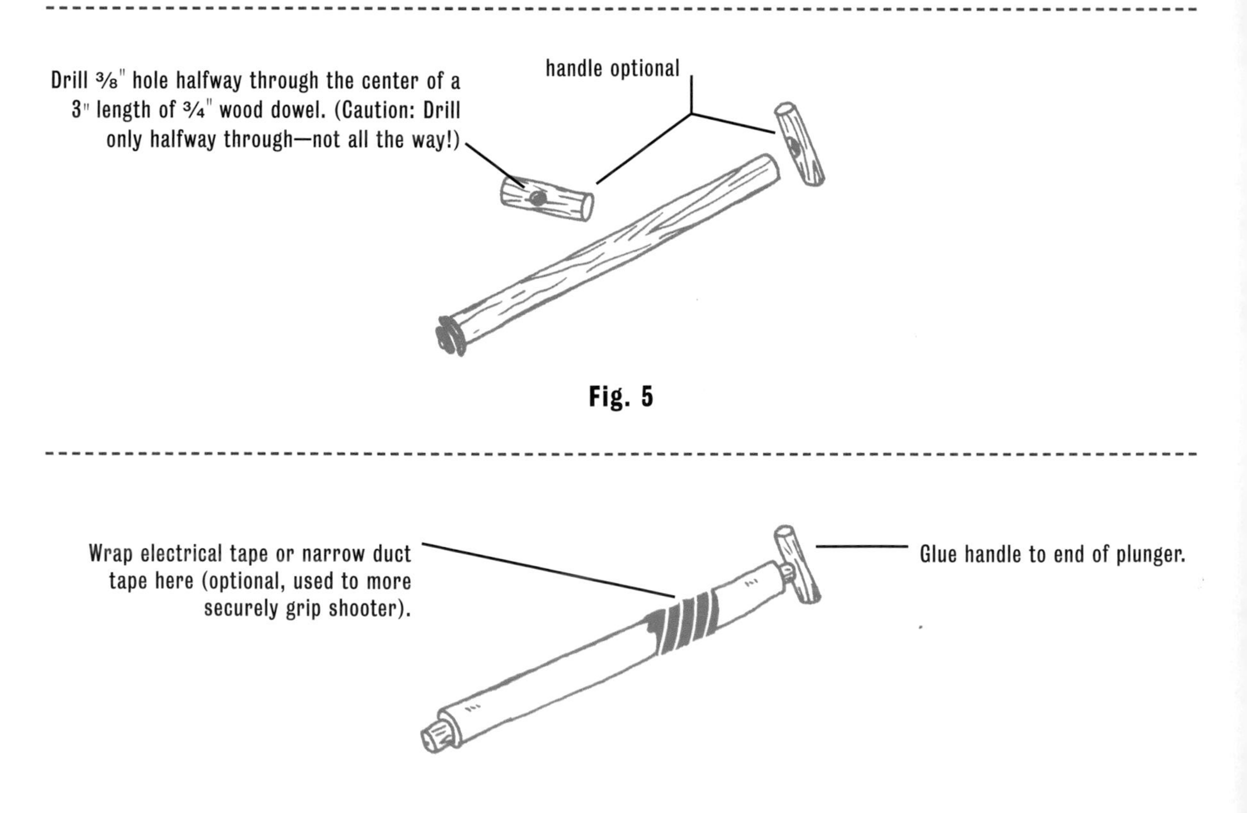


**Fig. 5**

**Fig. 6**

## 3 FILLING THE SHOOTER WITH WATER

1. Fill a container such as an empty plastic gallon milk jug with clean water.
2. Push the plunger into the pipe as far as it will go.
3. Stick the nozzle into the water and slowly pull the plunger back. This will "load" the shooter with water. *Caution:* Don't pull the plunger all the way out of the pipe!

## 4 USING THE SUPER-DUPER WATER SHOOTER

To shoot water, simply give the plunger a little jerk. Depending how hard and far you push the plunger each time you shoot, you can get from five to ten shots per load. In addition to being able to shoot farther than a garden-variety squirt gun, the Super-Duper Water Shooter can be filled in three to five seconds—even faster if you make a bigger hole in the nozzle. The "shooter" will work better if you keep a bit of petroleum jelly on the washer.

## 5 MODIFYING THE SHOOTER

If you want to really "soak" somebody every time you shoot, enlarge the nozzle's hole to 5⁄64" or 4⁄32". A larger hole will let you fill the "shooter" faster, but you won't have as many shots per fill-up!

**Important: Use clean water only in all water guns as well as the Super-Duper Water Shooter. Not only is it healthier, but it will also keep the nozzle from becoming plugged.**

# DRINKING-STRAW DISPENSER

Project 11

**Adult Supervision Required**
**Use of hacksaw, drill.**

**Have you ever picked a drinking straw out of an already-opened box and found your straw's end full of yuck? This fun-to-make straw dispenser keeps straws nearly germ free—even after grubby little hands have grabbed straws from it! All you do to get a clean straw from this dispenser is pull up its top and grab a straw. The dispenser automatically arranges the straws so it's easy to grab one without touching another one! It really works!**

## WHAT YOU NEED

- one empty potato chip container with lid (wash before using)
- two ½" #6 wood screws
- two small washers
- one 8½" length of a 2"-diameter wood dowel (use a fine-toothed hacksaw to make the cut)
- a section of plastic from the top of a plastic whipped-cream or margarine container
- one sheet of 8½" × 11" paper to cover container (optional)
- adhesive tape to secure paper to container (optional)
- and, of course, drinking straws

# 1 MAKING IT

1. First, use a marking pen and draw a 2¾" circle on the piece of plastic. This is the bottom of the dowel assembly. (One way to do this is to cut a piece from another potato chip container for a circle pattern. Another way to draw a circle is with a compass.)
2. Use a 3/32" drill bit and drill holes in the exact center of both ends of the 8" length of wood dowel. Using the same drill bit, drill holes in the exact center of the potato chip lid and the plastic circular bottom. Finding the exact center of the lid is simple—it has a small raised dot in its center. (One way to find the center of the lid, if it doesn't have a raised dot, is to use a ruler to draw three lines through the widest points of the circle. If you do it right, all the lines should meet at one point—the center. See **Fig. 1**.
3. Attach the lid to one end of the wood dowel with a ½"-long #6 wood screw and a small washer. See **Fig. 2**. Similarly, attach the plastic bottom to the dowel's other end.
4. Now insert the completed dowel assembly into the can and fill the can with straws. When you want a straw, simply grab the lid and pull up the assembly about halfway. This makes it easy to get one straw out of the dispenser without touching any of the other straws. Even though this dispenser will help keep straws clean, you should always wash your hands before eating or drinking.

Cut a 2¾" plastic circle from the lid of a margarine or other container. Using a ruler, draw three lines through the circle. The center of the circle is where the lines meet.

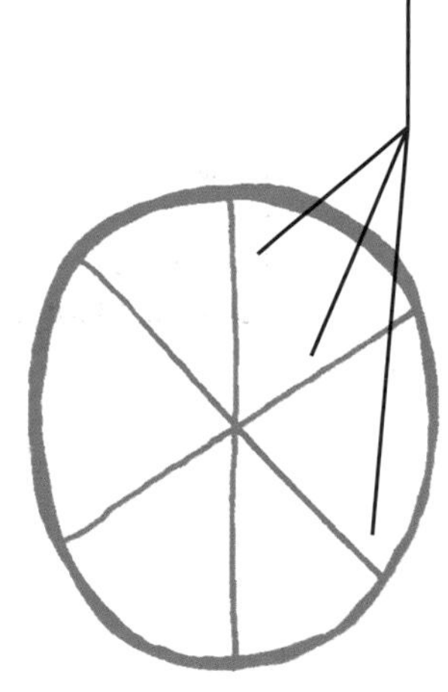

**Fig. 1**

# 2 GIVE THE STRAW DISPENSER A MAKEOVER

To change the appearance of your potato chip can—dress it up a little—all you need do is wrap a piece of 8½" × 11" paper around it. Some adhesive tape will hold the paper in place. You can use plain white paper, colored paper, or construction paper. But smooth, colored, copier paper looks best, and you can add stickers to make the straw dispenser look as neat as it works!

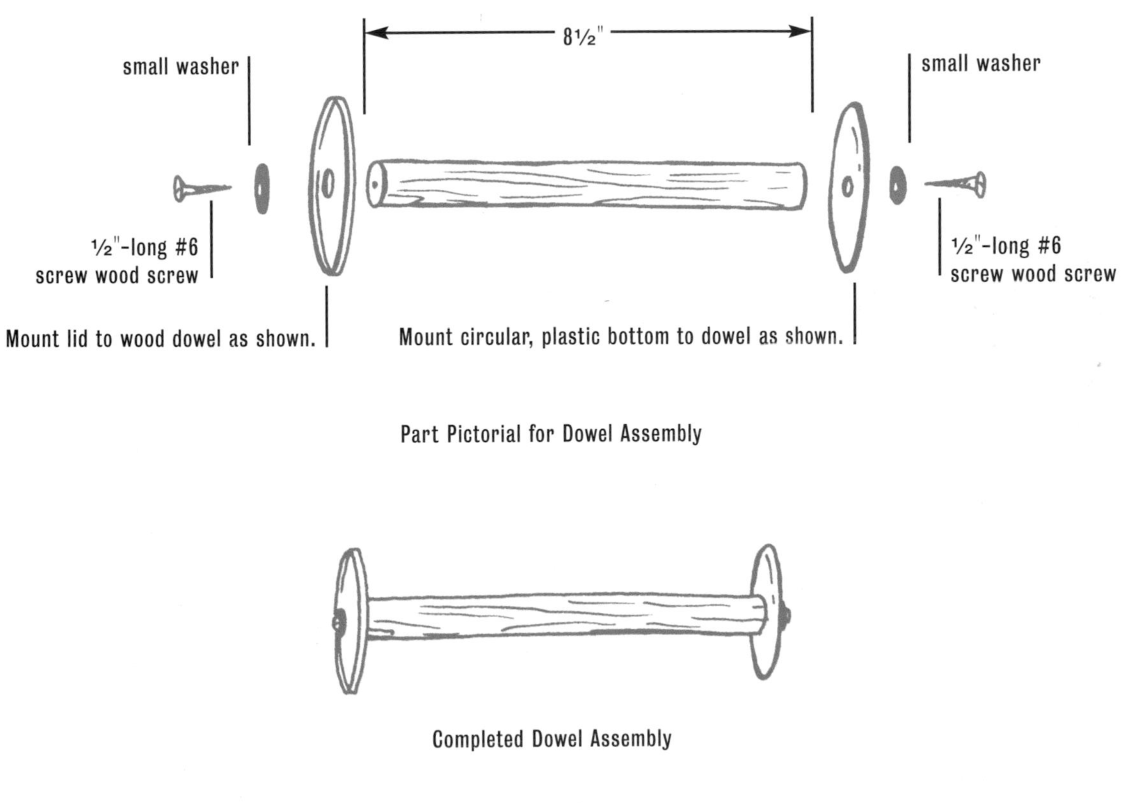


**Fig. 2**

# HIDDEN COMPARTMENT DISPLAY CASE

Project 12

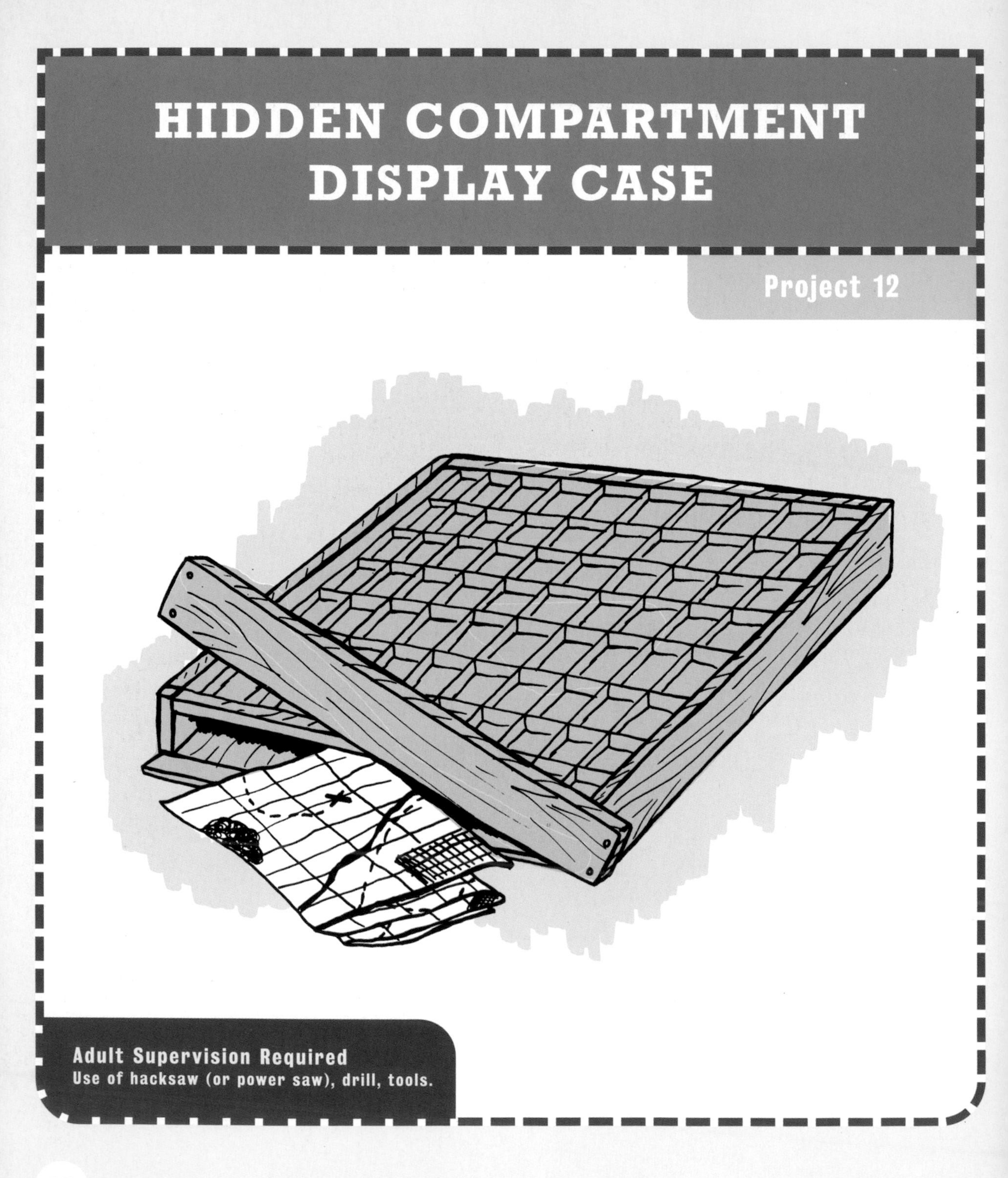

**Adult Supervision Required**
Use of hacksaw (or power saw), drill, tools.

One of the things that makes a trip or walk fun is bringing back cool stuff. The "find" could be a pretty leaf, an acorn, or something really cool like an old bottle cap!

But what do you do with it? Put it on your dresser until it's thick with dust? Here is a "neat" (in every sense of the word) place to put stuff so you can find and look at it anytime you want. If you collect small stones or coins, this display case is perfect for you, too. It even has a secret compartment—for baseball cards or a treasure map!

## WHAT YOU NEED

- one 12" × 12" piece of Plexiglas (clear top)
- one 12" × 12" piece of ¼" plywood (layout board)
- one 13" × 13½" piece of ¼" plywood (bottom)
- four 12" lengths of a ⅛" wood dowel—with one side flattened slightly with a file
- two 12" lengths of a 1 × 2 board (for sides)
- one 13" length of a 1× 2 board (back/secret door)
- one 13" length of a ¾" × 1¼" board (a 1 × 2 with ½" cut off its height (for front)*
- twelve 3" lengths of craft sticks with the rounded ends cut off
- forty-five 2¼" pieces of craft sticks with flat (not rounded) ends
- eight craft sticks (support for layout board)
- four 1" #6 wood screws
- thirteen ¾" #6 wood screws (four used merely to "fool" people)
- two 1" #8 roundhead wood screws
- four rubber feet (optional)
- wood glue and/or tacky glue
- small C-clamps
- several rubber bands (to hold board while glue dries)

*This can be done with a hacksaw, but someone with a power saw can do this for you much quicker and easier.

## 1 MAKING IT

Due to the complexity of this project, you will likely need to have an adult help you.

1. Check that wood pieces are cut to the lengths given above. Craft sticks can be cut with a sturdy pair of scissors.
2. Glue the flat side of the wood dowels to the sideboards as shown in **Fig. 2**. Use small C-clamps to hold them in place until the glue dries.
3. As shown in **Fig. 2**, glue the craft sticks (eight) to the sides, two glued-together pair to each side. These craft sticks will support the "layout board" for your display.
4. Use four 1½"-long #6 wood screws to fasten the 13½" length of a ¾" × 1¼" board to the front of the case (see **Fig. 1**).
5. Glue the layout board to the craft stick supports as shown in **Fig. 2**. Use rubber bands to hold it secure until the glue dries.
6. Use nine ¾" #6 wood screws to fasten the bottom to the case. See **Fig. 2**. Four rubber feet can be glued to bottom if desired.
7. Use **Fig. 3** as a guide to make holes where shown for the back, which also serves as the "secret door" for the "secret compartment." Use a small file to join the large and small holes.
8. The trick to making the "secret door" a success is to make sure that the holes for the two wood screws are lined up exactly with the two small holes in the bottom. See **Fig. 3**.
9. Use tacky glue to fasten the twelve 3¾" and forty-five 2¼" pieces of craft sticks to the layout board as shown in **Fig. 1**.
10. Drill a small hole near the front of the Plexiglas and tie on a small piece of shoestring. The shoestring will make it easy to open.

## 2 USING IT

In addition to a place to keep the neat stuff you find, you can use this display to store one hundred state quarters. There is room to show both the front and back of each state quarter. The "secret compartment" is perfect for hiding really valuable stuff from prying eyes!

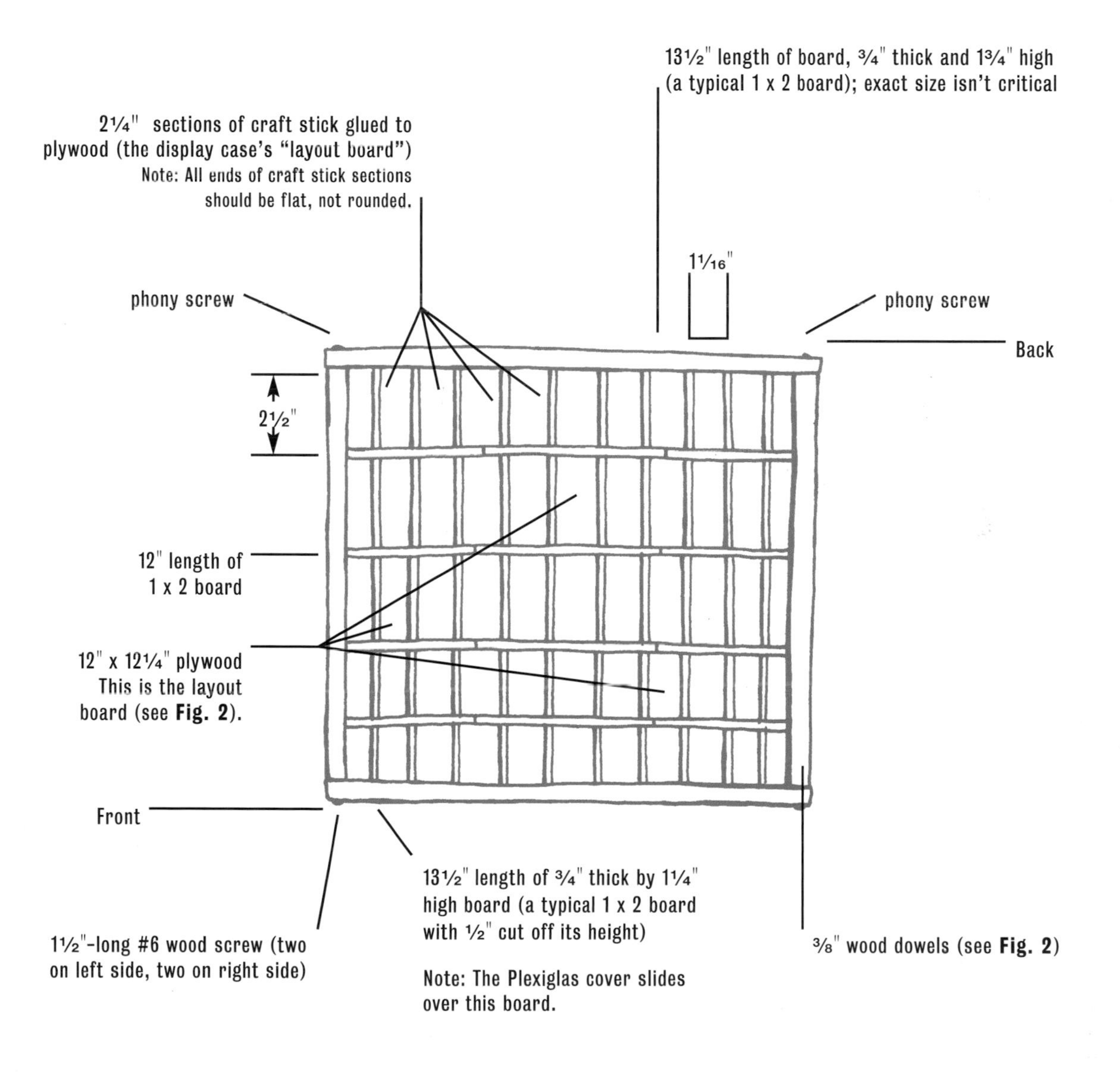

**Fig. 1**

Top View

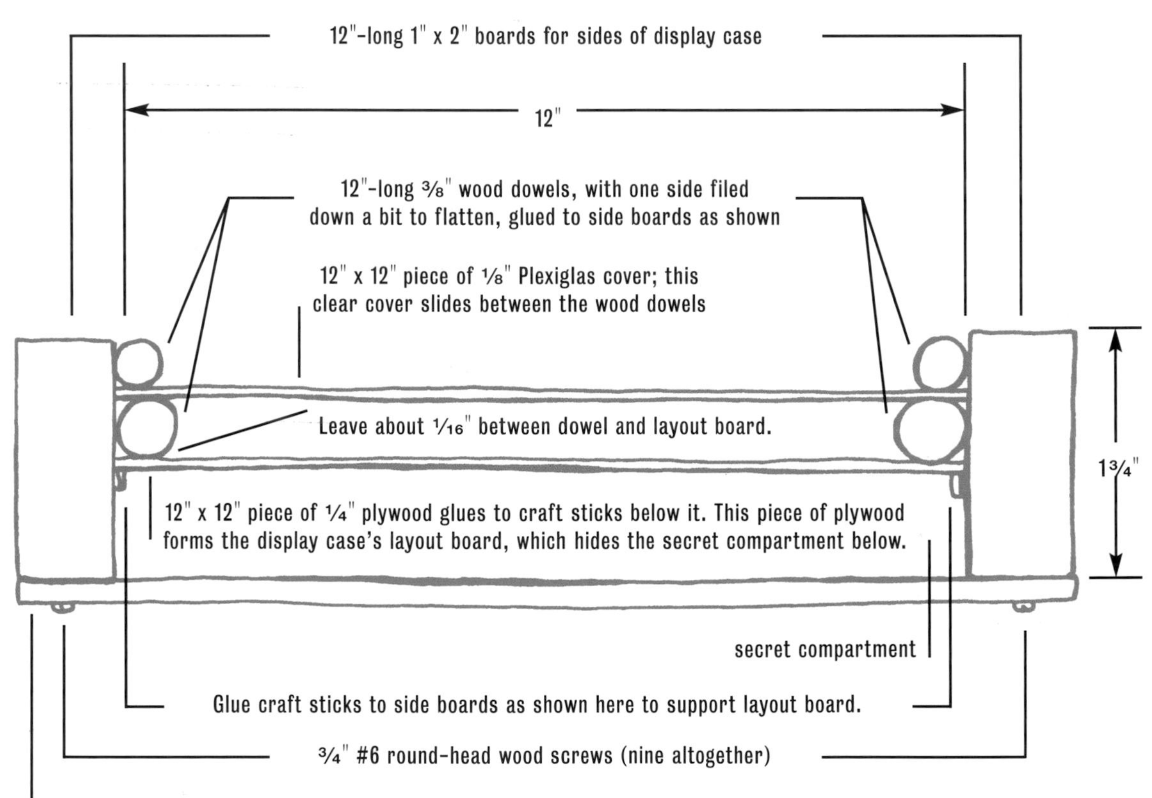


**Fig. 2**

Front View

Note: Front and back boards and inside partition not shown.

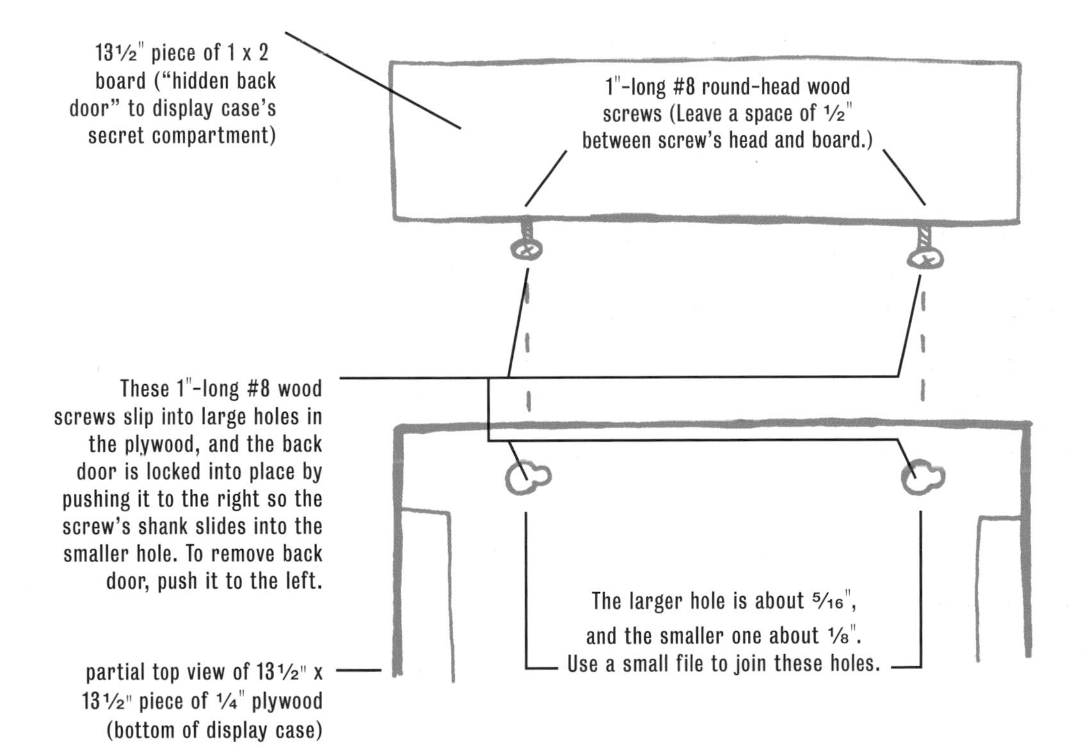


**Fig. 3**

Top View of Bottom Board

Note: Only back part of board is shown.

# SOLAR-POWERED POCKET WATCH

Project 13

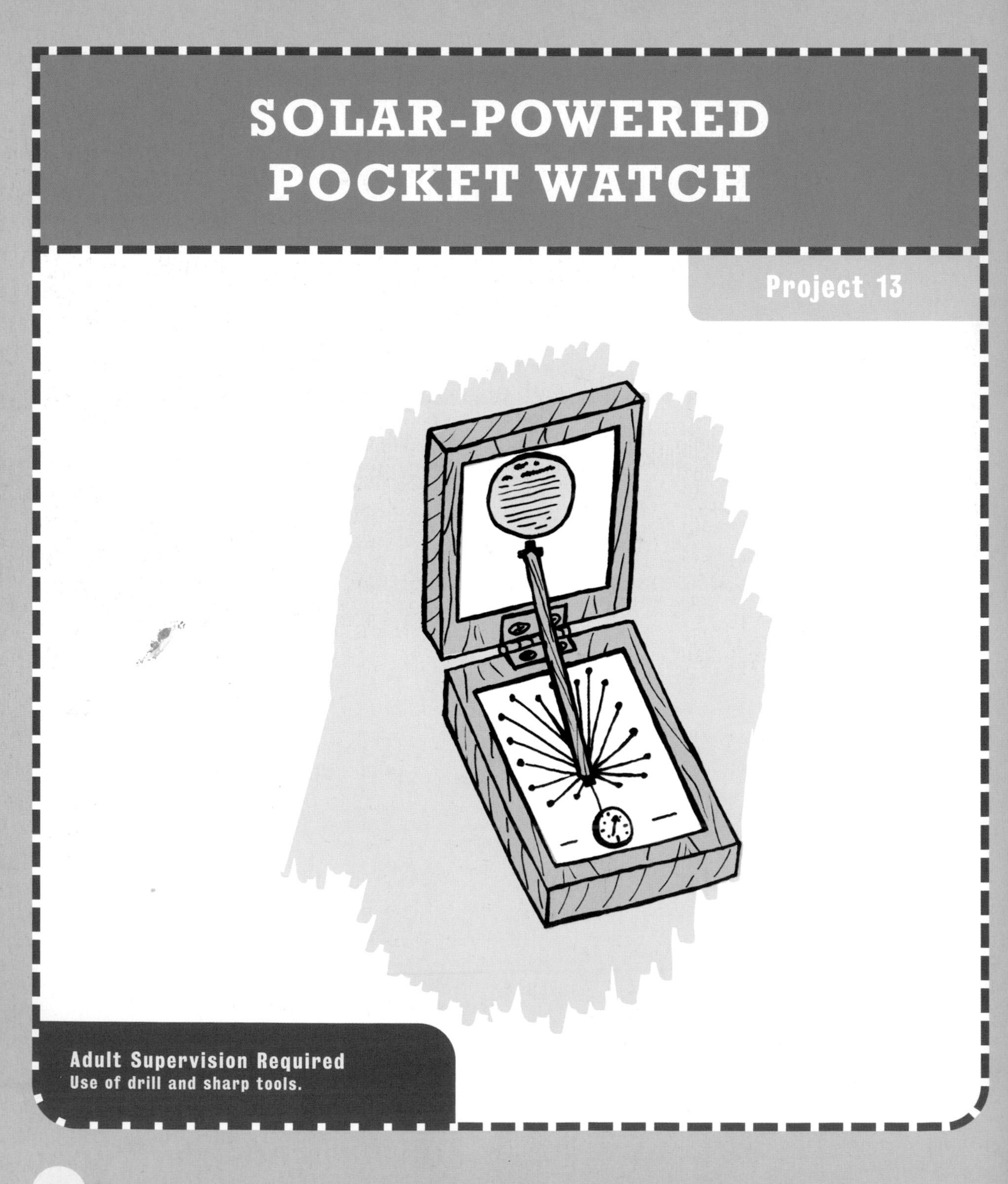

**Adult Supervision Required**
Use of drill and sharp tools.

It keeps going and going and going! Century after century, it keeps perfect time. It doesn't use a battery or need winding, and you can take it with you on a hike! What is it? A pocket sundial!

The science of sundials is called "agnomics." By the way, "gnomon" is the name given to the part of a sundial that casts the shadow.

The project described here is meant to be carried in a backpack or large pocket. It uses a tiny compass so it can be oriented properly with the sun. To use the pocket sundial, you open it up, hold it level, and then turn it so that the compass's North needle points to a mark on the faceplate. Then you simply read off the time!

## WHAT YOU NEED

- one 5¼" length of a 1 × 4 board
- one 4½" length of a 1 × 4 board
- one 1" length of a 1 × 4 board
- two 4½"-long pieces of a ⅜"-diameter wood dowel
- one 2<sup></sup>13/16" length of a ⅜"-diameter wood dowel
- one 4½" length of a 3/16"-diameter wood dowel (for gnomon)
- one small hinge (about 1¼" to 2" long)
- four ½"-long #6 wood screws
- two 1¼"-long #6 wood screws
- one tiny compass
- wood glue
- latch (optional)
- water-based sealer (optional)

Note: Remember, 1 × 4 boards are actually ¾" × 3½".

## 1 MAKING IT

1. Slightly flatten one side of each dowel with a wood file. This will allow the pieces of dowels hold better to the base.
2. Using **Fig.** 1 as a guide, glue the pieces of 3⁄8" wood dowels to the base.
3. Using **Fig.** 2 as a guide, use a small file to make a groove on a 1"-wide piece of a 1 × 4 board so a small hinge can be attached to it. (See also **Fig.** 3.) After you have made the groove, glue this piece to the base as shown. For additional strength, you can use two wood screws as shown.
4. Using **Fig.** 3 as a guide, attach hinge to cover and base, as shown, with four 1⁄2"-long #6 wood screws.
5. Photocopy (or trace) the templates on pages 70 and 71 and cut out the copies of the templates at the dashed lines. Glue Template 1 to inside of cover. Line up the top of the template with the top of the cover before gluing. Glue Template 2 to base. Use a hobby knife or similar tool to make notches in the cover and base where shown in the templates. These notches support the gnomon. Glue a tiny compass to Template 2 where indicated. A 41⁄2" length of a 1⁄8"- or 3⁄16"-diameter wood dowel is used for the gnomon. Store this gnomon diagonally in the base of the sundial when not in use. If desired, a small latch can be used for the cover.

For long life, protect templates with several coats of a *water-based* sealer, which is available in craft supply stores.

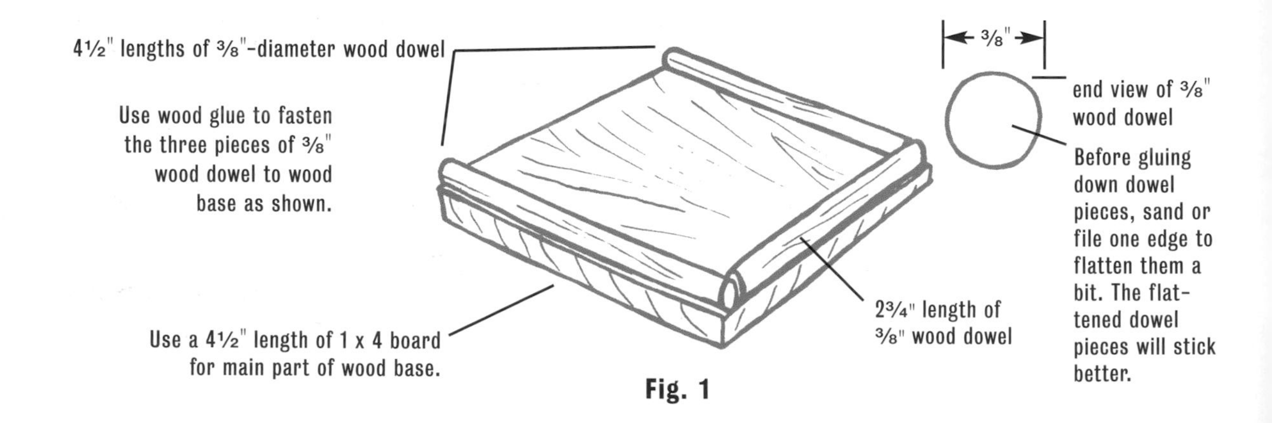


**Fig. 1**

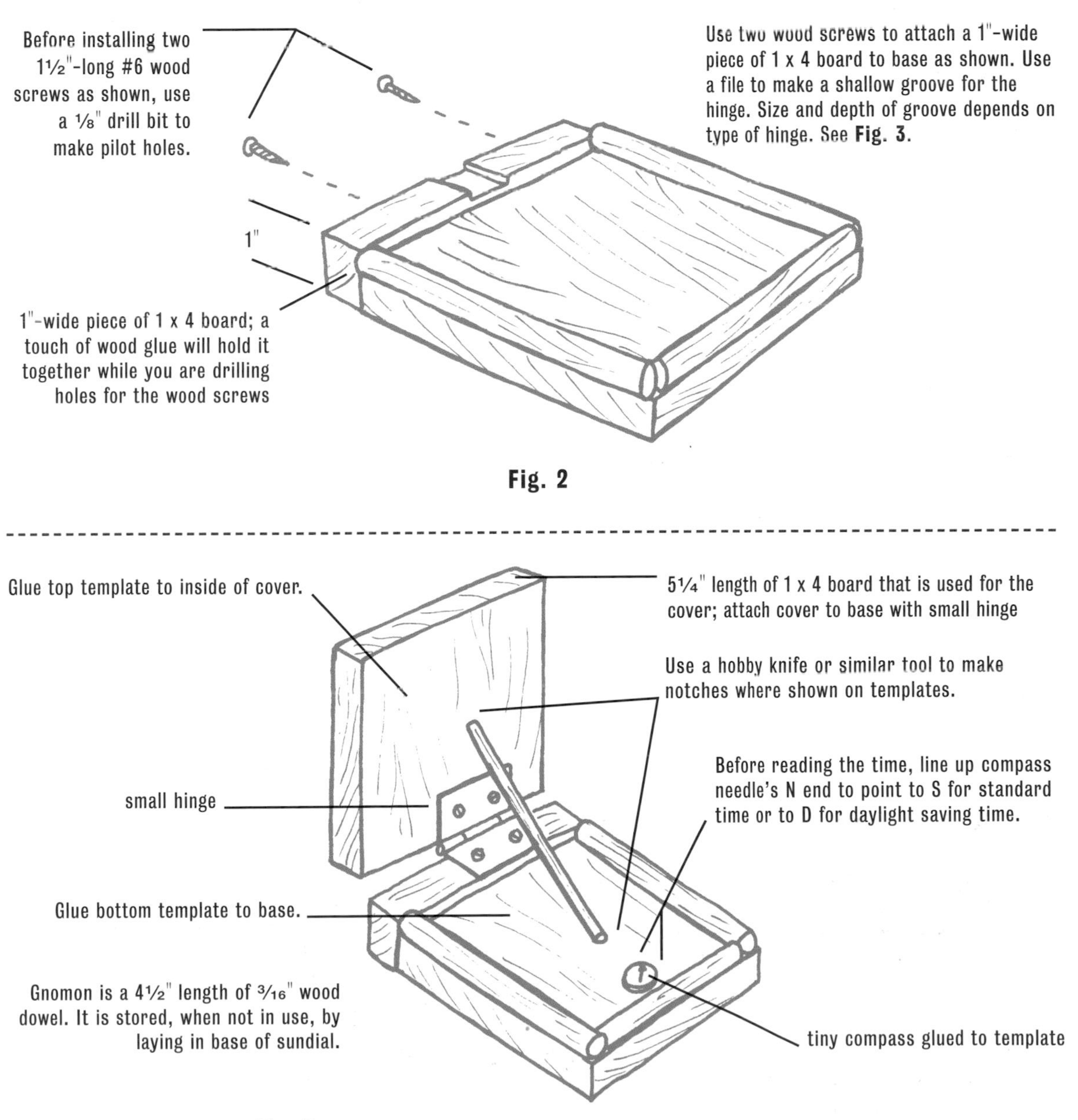
Before installing two
1½"-long #6 wood
screws as shown, use
a ⅛" drill bit to
make pilot holes.
Use two wood screws to attach a 1"-wide piece of 1 x 4 board to base as shown. Use a file to make a shallow groove for the hinge. Size and depth of groove depends on type of hinge. See **Fig. 3**.
1"
1"-wide piece of 1 x 4 board; a touch of wood glue will hold it together while you are drilling holes for the wood screws

**Fig. 2**

Glue top template to inside of cover.
5¼" length of 1 x 4 board that is used for the cover; attach cover to base with small hinge
Use a hobby knife or similar tool to make notches where shown on templates.
Before reading the time, line up compass needle's N end to point to S for standard time or to D for daylight saving time.
small hinge
Glue bottom template to base.
Gnomon is a 4½" length of 3/16" wood dowel. It is stored, when not in use, by laying in base of sundial.
tiny compass glued to template

**Fig. 3**

## 2 CALIBRATION

In order for your sundial to give accurate time, it must be calibrated. This is best done at noon on a sunny day. Take the sundial outside, open it up, and position the gnomon in the notches. With the sundial held level, turn it so that the shadow from the gnomon shows the correct time. Now place a pencil or pen mark on the bottom template where the compass's North needle points. If you are on standard time, label this mark "S." Label it "D" if you are on daylight saving time. Repeat this procedure when there is a time change (from standard to daylight saving or vice versa).

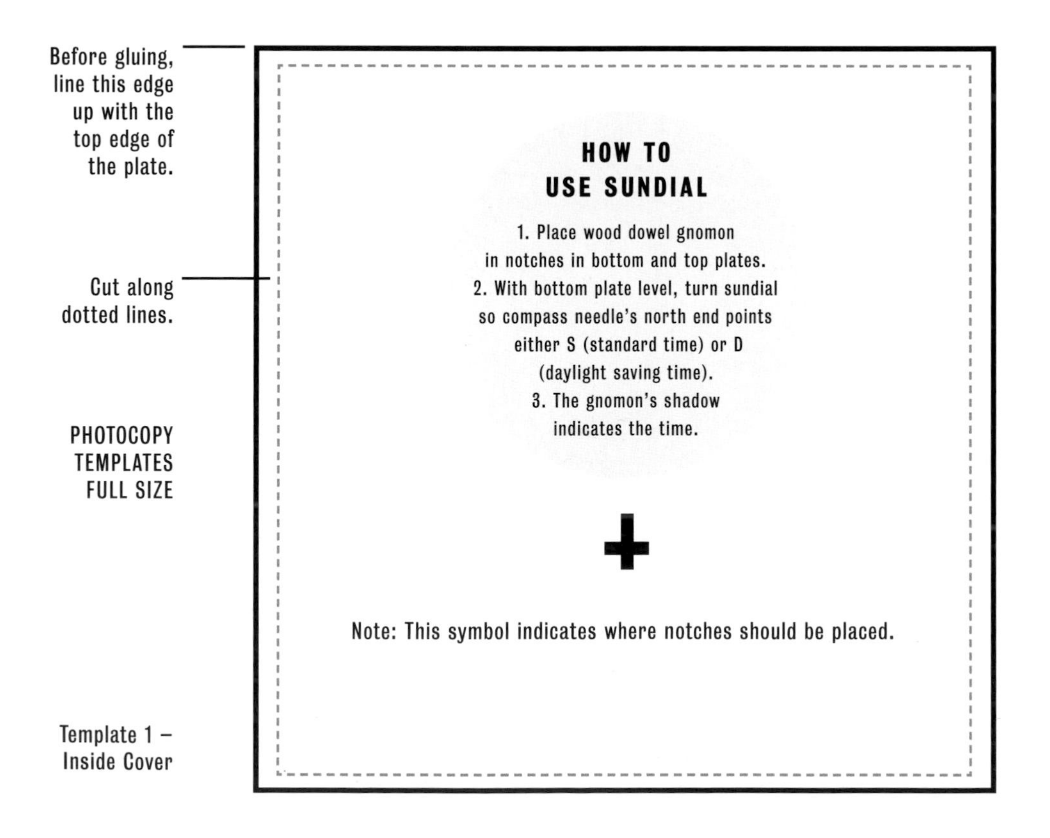

# 3 USING IT

To use the Solar-Powered Pocket Watch, follow the directions printed on the inside of the cover. While the day must be sunny in order to tell time with it, the pocket sundial is useful whenever you take a hike because its built-in compass will help keep you from getting lost.

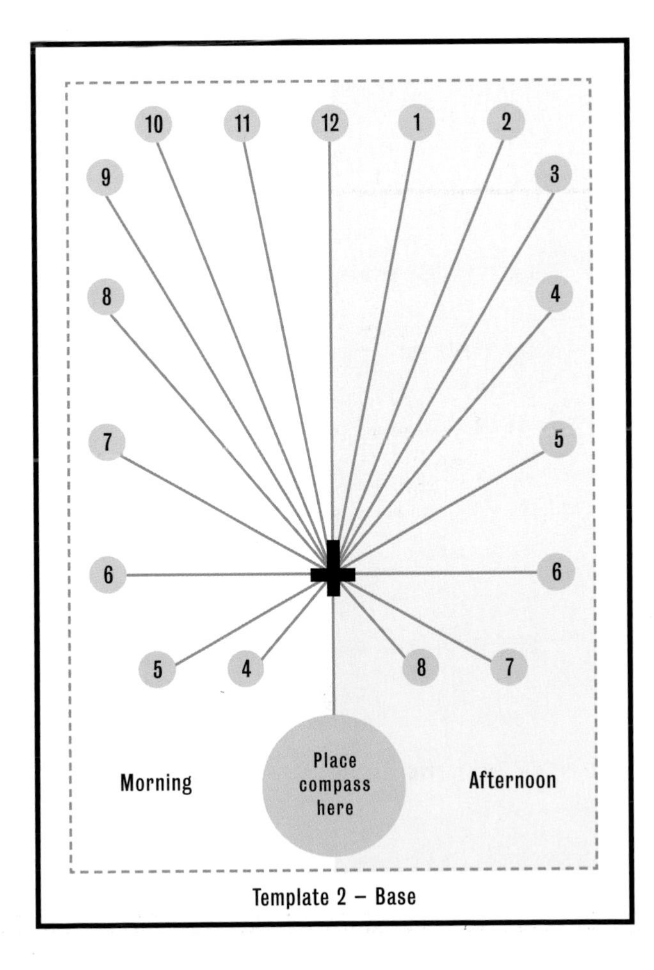

Template 2 – Base

# IT'S ELECTRIFYING!

The remaining projects in this book use electricity. With electrical gadgets such as TVs, radios, lights, and computers so common, it's assumed that people who design this amazing stuff understand electricity completely. The truth is that electricity is still mysterious, even to professional electronic designers, such as myself.

Before you read further, find two similar magnets and play with them awhile. It's amazing what one can learn about electricity by playing with magnets. In fact, electricity and magnetism are so closely related that many scientists consider them basically the same. Once you get your hands on two similar magnets, try putting them together in various ways to see what happens. Put together one way, you'll notice that they are attracted to each other. They actually seem to stick together as if they're glued. This happens only when the opposite poles of the two magnets come together (all magnets have positive and negative poles). Move the magnets around some more and you will find that, in another position, they repel each other. In fact, if the magnets are powerful enough (like the expensive Neodymium types), you would have to have superstrength to be able to put the two magnets together so their same poles actually touch each other!

Despite the mystery of what electricity really is, we know at least enough to partially explain some odd happenings, such as the results of a simple experiment I did with my son Mark some years ago (see Comb and Tissue Experiment, pages 76–77). But now, let's take a quick look at some things scientists know about electricity.

Scientists are pretty sure that all matter consists of tiny particles called atoms. Atoms, in turn, consist of other even smaller particles—primarily neutrons, protons, and electrons. Electrons are charged with negative electricity and protons are charged with positive electricity. However, neutrons are not charged at all. Keep in mind that negatively charged stuff repels negatively charged stuff and positively charged stuff repels positively charged stuff. However, negatively charged stuff is attracted to positively charged stuff. Stuff that isn't charged isn't affected by charged stuff at all. This is basically what happens between two magnets.

If you took my earlier suggestion about playing with two similar magnets, you should have a working understanding of what happens between electrically charged stuff. As for what happens between charged stuff and uncharged stuff, try picking up a small piece of wood with a magnet! What happens? Nothing at all! (Unless, of course, there's a steel nail in the wood; then *maybe* the magnet would pick it up.)

Experiments seem to show that protons and neutrons are stuck together in the center of the atom, held together by something called "the nuclear force." This center of the atom is called the nucleus. Electrons circle the nucleus a good distance from it. It is similar to the way the earth and planets circle the sun, or the Space Shuttle and satellites circle the earth. Some of the electrons farthest from the center of the atom can move from atom to atom. The protons in the nucleus are much heavier than the electrons and are really hard to move. The tiny little electrons circling far from the nucleus are very light, so can be made to move around easily. All they need is a little "nudge" from an electrical force. The designers of electrical gadgets depend on the fact that electrons can be made to move easily when they work with some types of metals.

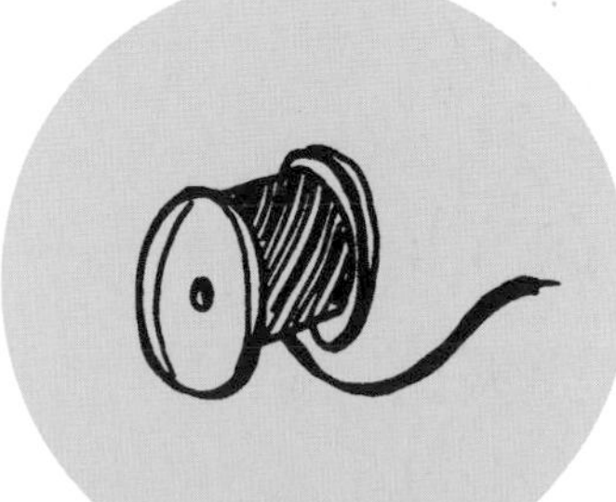

## WIRING TIPS AND HINTS

Electrical wire is usually made of copper (which is the color of a shiny penny) with a plastic coating on it. Electricity flows easily through copper but not through plastic. When using electrical wire to make connections, remove about ½" of plastic from the end of a wire before making the connection. Don't remove more than 1" of this insulation from each end of the wire. A tool called a wire stripper is often used to remove insulation at the ends of wires, but it can be done easily with a good pair of scissors if you're careful.

In this book, we'll show you how to make good connections by twisting wires together or around a screw and then taping them with a bit of duct tape. It's a good idea to test your connection by pulling on the wires slightly to make sure they don't come apart. Better connections are made with solder, but soldering should be done only under the guidance of an adult.

One of the most common problems when making something that uses electricity is bad connections. Metal must be in contact with metal for electricity to flow. The shinier the metal used, the better. Keep this in mind if you run into problems with any project that uses electricity.

## MAGNET WIRE

Magnet wire is commonly used to make electromagnets. Don't get confused, though. Electricity flowing in any type of wire will create magnetism. Magnet wire, however, is special since its insulation is a very thin varnish-type coating. While any type of wire creates magnetism, magnet wire is the best to use when you want to make an electromagnet! Electric motors, electric starters, and electric generators all use magnet wire because they work on the principle of electromagnetism.

## EXPERIMENTER BREADBOARD

A small version of this neat wiring helper is used in Project 20 in this book. Large experimenter breadboards can be used to wire complicated circuits such as computers. Drawing BREADBOARD shows the top view of the small board we use in the project. An experimenter breadboard can be used over and over again.

## HINTS ON USING EXPERIMENTER BREADBOARDS

The wire leads of electronic parts such as transistors and resistors are inserted in the holes in the breadboard. The breadboard is made in such a way so that the five holes in a column, on each side of the board, are connected electrically even though you can't see the connections. Also, the long lines of holes on the outside of the board are connected. See the drawing BREADBOARD.

Wires used in all projects in this book are insulated. Most are insulated with colored plastic, although magnet wire is insulated with a thin, nearly invisible varnish-type coating. Before making any connections or before inserting a wire in a hole in an experimenter breadboard, remove around ½" of insulation from each end. With plastic coated wires this can be done with wire strippers, side cutters, or even a good, sturdy pair of scissors. Fine sandpaper works best with magnet wire. When wiring, it is best to use as many different colored wires as possible since this makes wiring simpler. Remember, only the "insulation" is colored. The metal in the center of the wire is not colored.

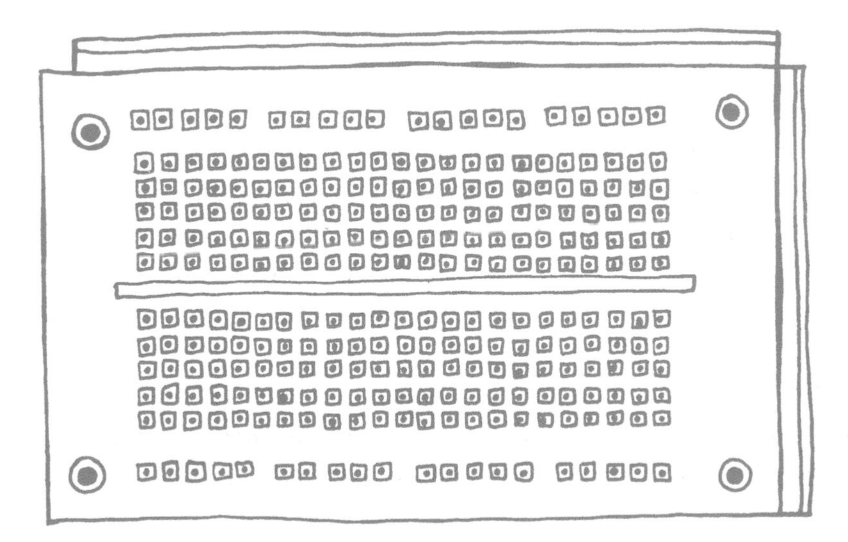

**BREADBOARD**

# COMB AND TISSUE EXPERIMENT

Tiny bits of tissue paper lay on a table. As my son Mark looked on, I passed a hard plastic comb through my hair a few times, then moved the comb near the bits of tissue. When the comb neared the tissue bits, a tiny piece of tissue suddenly jumped on the comb. Fifteen seconds later, it suddenly flew off! My son shook his head and asked, "Why did it do that?"

"Did you notice, Mark, that I used the comb on my hair?"

"Yes, Dad, I saw that."

"What if I didn't use the comb?" I said.

"Hmm, let me see." Mark picked up another comb and tried the same trick. After a minute or two he yelled, "Hey, Dad. I did it!" Jokingly, Mark had placed some tissue bits on the comb, but they quickly fell off. His comb didn't attract the tissue at all.

"What do you think is going on?" I asked with a smile.

"It's static electricity. Right, Dad!" he stated, as if that completely answered the question.

"Yes," I agreed slowly. "When a comb passes through hair, some electrons in the hair move to the comb. Since electrons are negatively charged, the comb then becomes negatively charged." I paused for a moment. "But why does the comb attract the uncharged tissue? Don't only oppositely charged things attract each other?"

"Well, Dad, maybe positively charged protons move towards the negatively charged comb and then the tissue bit moves."

**Fig. 1** Unrubbed comb has same number of electrons and protons, so comb has no electrical charge.

**Fig. 2** As comb passes through hair, electrons from hair move to comb. Comb then has a negative electric charge.

**Fig. 3** Note: Comb is tilted. After comb goes through hair, it is negatively charged. Bits of tissue are not electrically charged.

**Fig. 4** Note: Comb is tilted. As negatively charged comb nears bits of tissue, one of the bits is attracted to the comb. Let's take a closer look.

"Mark," I said, "protons are big and heavy, and really hard to move. More likely what's going on is that the light electrons are repelled to the opposite side of the tissue while the heavy, positively charged protons just sit there. With fewer electrons on the side of the tissue close to the comb, and the same number of positive protons as before, a positive charge develops on the side of the tissue closest to the comb." Since my son seemed to be following that, I continued. "This positive side of the tissue is then attracted to the negatively charged comb. Because the force isn't enough to pull the tissue apart, the whole tissue moves."

"Okay, Dad, but why does the tissue bit shoot off? Do the electrons move back again closer to the protons?"

"If that were happening, the tissue would just fall off. Since the tissue bit shot off, there must be repulsion taking place. Some of the electrons on the comb move into the tissue, and the whole tissue becomes negatively charged. Since now both comb and tissue are negatively charged, they repel each other." After catching my breath I asked, "Why do you suppose the tissue shoots off the comb, and not the comb off the tissue? They repel each other, don't they?"

"Well, Dad, the comb is so big and the tissue is so small. It's like when a big bully pushes a tiny but spunky kid who pushes back—it's the little kid who winds up on the ground and the bully is still standing!"

"You've got it, Mark!"

In this close-up, notice that the negatively charged comb has repelled electrons in the tissue. This causes the side closest to the comb to become positively charged. **Fig. 5**

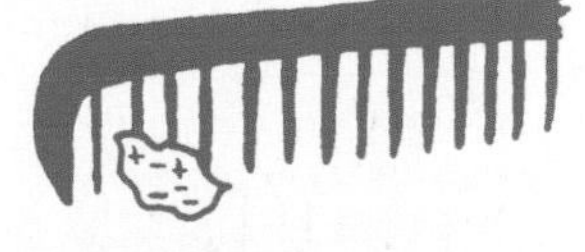

Now some negatively charged electrons on the comb have moved into the bit of tissue, and the tissue has moved slightly. **Fig. 6**

Here are the comb and the bit of tissue about 10 seconds after the tissue first jumped to the comb (compare to **Fig. 5**). **Fig. 7**

Here are the comb and the bit of tissue about 15 seconds after the tissue jumped to the comb (compare to **Fig. 5**). Notice that the bit of tissue is now negatively charged and is being repelled by the negatively charged comb. **Fig. 8**

# MOBILE THUNDERSTORM DETECTOR

Project 14

Be honest—would you go on a long hike or bike ride or out fishing if a thunderstorm was coming? I wouldn't. So what can you do? Listen carefully to the weather forecast before venturing out? Should you cancel an outing just because the forecast says there's a chance of thunderstorms? Do this and, at least in some areas, you may never get out for a long hike or day's fishing in the summer. Talk about a downer! Then what do you do? Cancel everything just because a weather report says there is a chance of a thunder-shower? No way! So do what I do. What I do is listen to my mobile thunderstorm detector, my AM radio!

## WHAT YOU NEED

- AM radio

# 1 USING YOUR AM RADIO TO DETECT THUNDERSTORMS

Everyone knows lightning makes light and lots of it. It also makes an exceptionally loud sound. What you might not know is that lightning makes radio waves as well! These waves are just like the ones radio stations produce. You have probably even picked up these radio waves on your AM radio. They make a scratching, sizzling noise. When loud, it can sound like an egg dropped into a scorching-hot frying pan. The common term for this noise on the radio is "static." While other things, even a nearby loose lightbulb, can create static on the radio, radio noise made by lightning is special. Scientists refer to this radio noise as "atmospherics," or "sferics" for short.

In order to hear static, you will need an AM radio. Nearly all small portable radios are either just AM or both AM and FM. For several reasons, FM radio doesn't pick up static well. Only AM radios should be used to detect thunderstorms.

Tune your radio to a weak station or a blank spot—one without a station. Ideally, you should tune it to the low part of the dial—below 1000. Now you will have to wait. In much of the country, even in summer, it may be a week or longer before you will hear static on the radio during the day. However, you may be able to hear static nearly every summer night. The reason for this is that radio waves travel farther at night, so you pick up the static from thunderstorms hundreds of miles away. During the day, about a hundred miles away is about as far as you can detect a thunderstorm with a radio.

Some summer night, tune an AM receiver to a weak station

and listen for noise. The noise you hear will likely be static made by lightning. If the noise is relatively weak, it is probably caused by lightning many hundreds of miles away. It is unlikely that you will be awakened that night by a thunderstorm. If the noise seems to be getting louder from hour to hour the thunderstorm may be moving toward you and you may be woken up by a crash of thunder.

## ELECTRIC POTENTIAL

The difference in electric potential between a comb with static electricity and a lightning strike is what is important and is commonly referred to as simply "voltage." Think of a water hose with water coming out. The higher the pressure of the water, the harder the water comes out. High enough pressure

**TAKE COVER!**

**Flash! Crackle! Crash! Boom! Boom! Bang! Roarrr! Thunderstorms can be scary. If you are in a building or car, sit back and enjoy nature's thrilling show—but stay off most land-line telephones during the storms (cordless ones are okay).**

**Cars are especially safe when lightning threatens. But being outside during a thunderstorm can be downright hazardous. Lightning can and does cause serious, even deadly, injuries.**

**What if you are on a long hike and you hear thunder? With that first sound of thunder, try to take shelter in a building or car. If you can't find that kind of shelter, crouch down in a low, protected spot. Don't be afraid to get down on your hands and knees, even if you get wet! Stay away from tall trees! Lightning bolts take the shortest route to the ground, so they love tall trees. For the same reason, don't make yourself into a target by being the highest point in the area—don't stand on a golf course or a flat open space during a thunderstorm, or sit in a small boat.**

**BEN FRANKLIN'S STORM-TELLING BELLS**

**A thunderstorm detector sounds a bit amazing, like high technology. But Benjamin Franklin made one in 1752, before the Revolutionary War. Ben referred to his device as "storm-telling bells," and it actually worked! Ben connected one end of a wire to one bell and the other end of the wire to a metal rod on his roof. The other bell was connected to a wire that he connected to his water well. When storm clouds neared, the difference in electrical potential (see sidebar) made the bells ring. The louder they rang, the closer the storm. Franklin found that the bells sometimes rang when there was no lightning or thunder, only a dark cloud over the rod.**

and you can break a window by just aiming the stream of water at it. The "pressure" here, when we talk about water, is similar to "voltage" when we talk about electricity. A 9-volt battery, which is perfectly safe, has less than a tenth as much "voltage" as the electricity in your wall, which is around 120 volts. This 120 volts can be dangerous if you aren't careful. Since a lightning stroke is measured in millions of volts, it is obvious why lightning is so dangerous. If you followed my dialogue with Mark on why the bit of tissue flew off the charged comb, you should be able to understand why Ben Franklin's storm-telling bells often worked. The first drawing here, **Fig.** 1, shows the basic setup. Notice that the metal rod on the roof picks up some of the negative charge from the cloud. This negative charge flows through the wire to one of the bells, causing it to be negatively charged. The other bell is connected by a wire to the ground. The ground beneath storm clouds becomes positively charged because the negatively charged cloud pushes the electrons away from the ground beneath it. The metal ball, which has no charge before it touches a bell, is attracted to the negatively charged bell for the same reason the bit of tissue was first attracted to the comb. For more explanation, look at the other drawings here along with their captions, **Fig.** 2.

# STORM-TELLING BELLS

## WHY BEN FRANKLIN'S STORM-TELLING BELLS RANG

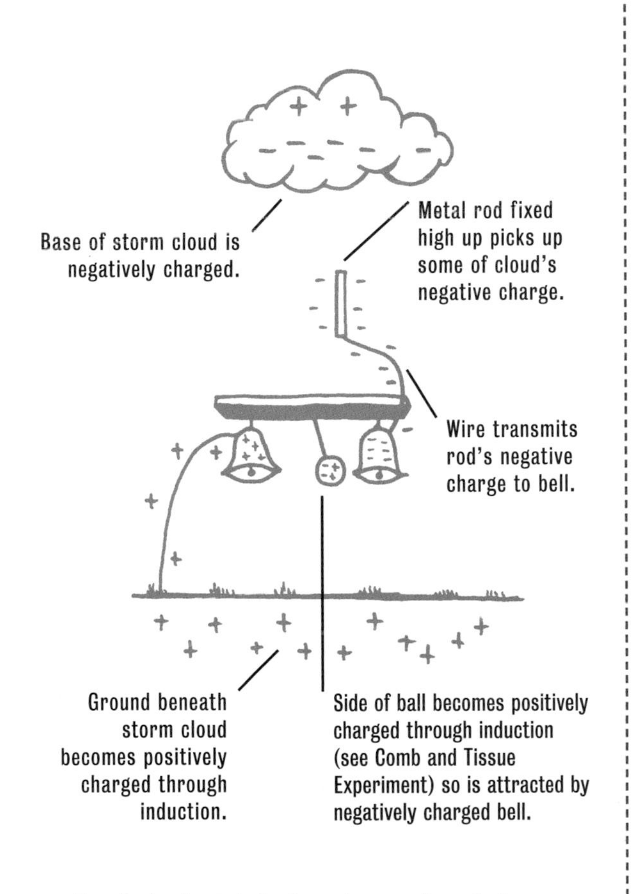


Negatively charged cloud repels many free electrons away from ground directly beneath storm cloud.

**Fig. 1**

Metal ball strikes negatively charged bell and picks up negative charge. It is then repelled by bell.

The now negatively charged ball is attracted to positively charged bell.

Metal ball strikes positively charged bell and gives up its negative charge for a positive charge. This process keeps repeating until the storm cloud passes by.

**Fig. 2**

# SIDEWINDER THINGAMAJIG

Project 15

**Adult Supervision Required**
Use of drill and tools.

What do sidewinder rattlesnakes and guided missiles have in common? The same thing as this project: they all can "see" some types of invisible infrared light! When invisible light hits this Sidewinder Thingamajig, a small red light goes on! It's obvious that this project is perfect for magic tricks. However, it has another, more practical use—it will help you check out all those remote controls around your home. An instrument similar to this is used by experts who repair electronics.

## WHAT YOU NEED

- one infrared phototransistor
- one red LED (an LED is a type of tiny light bulb; LED stands for light-emitting diode and is similar to a laser)
- one 9V battery connector
- one 9V battery
- one large craft stick
- duct tape
- epoxy cement (optional)

## 1 MAKING IT

1. Drill four 1⁄16" holes in a large craft stick as shown in **Fig. 1**.
2. Using **Fig. 2** as a guide, insert the leads from the phototransistor and LED in holes as shown. Make sure you insert the shorter leads in the indicated holes! These short leads are next to the flat sides. See also **Fig. 3**.
3. Turn over the craft stick and make connections as shown in **Fig. 4**. Use duct tape to make sure the leads don't untwist. Connect the battery connector's leads as indicated. Watch the colors of the wires here!
4. Use duct tape to hold the battery to the craft stick. A dab of epoxy cement can be used to glue the LED and phototransistor to the craft stick.

## 2 TESTING IT

Snap on the battery connector. With the lights off in the room, shine a flashlight on the phototransistor. The LED should light. If it doesn't, make sure your connections are good, the phototransistor and LED are installed correctly, and the battery is good.

## 3 USING IT

In a dimly lit or dark room, take a remote control unit that you know works well and, at a distance of less than a foot, point it at the Sidewinder Thingamajig's phototransistor. Press a button on the remote. While you can't see the remote control's invisible light, the Sidewinder Thingamajig can!

The Sidewinder Thingamajig is the perfect gadget to figure out why a remote that uses infrared light doesn't work. To check out your remote simply point it at the Sidewinder Thingamajig's phototransistor. Every button you press should light the LED. If nothing lights it, either the remote's battery is bad or the remote itself has had it. If every button causes the LED to light, but the TV or VCR doesn't respond, either the TV or VCR has problems or, more likely, you are using the wrong remote control!

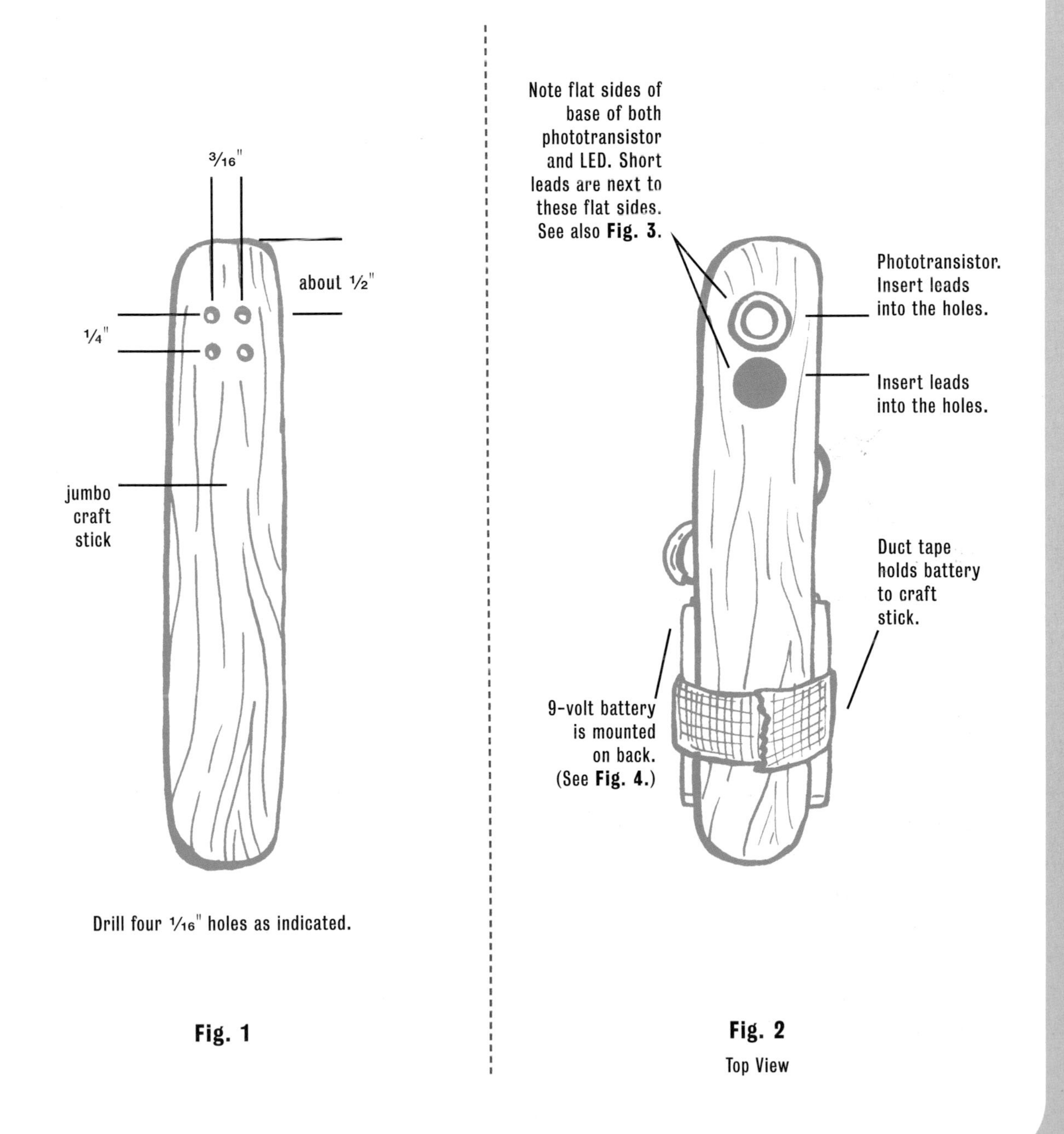


**Fig. 1**

**Fig. 2**
Top View

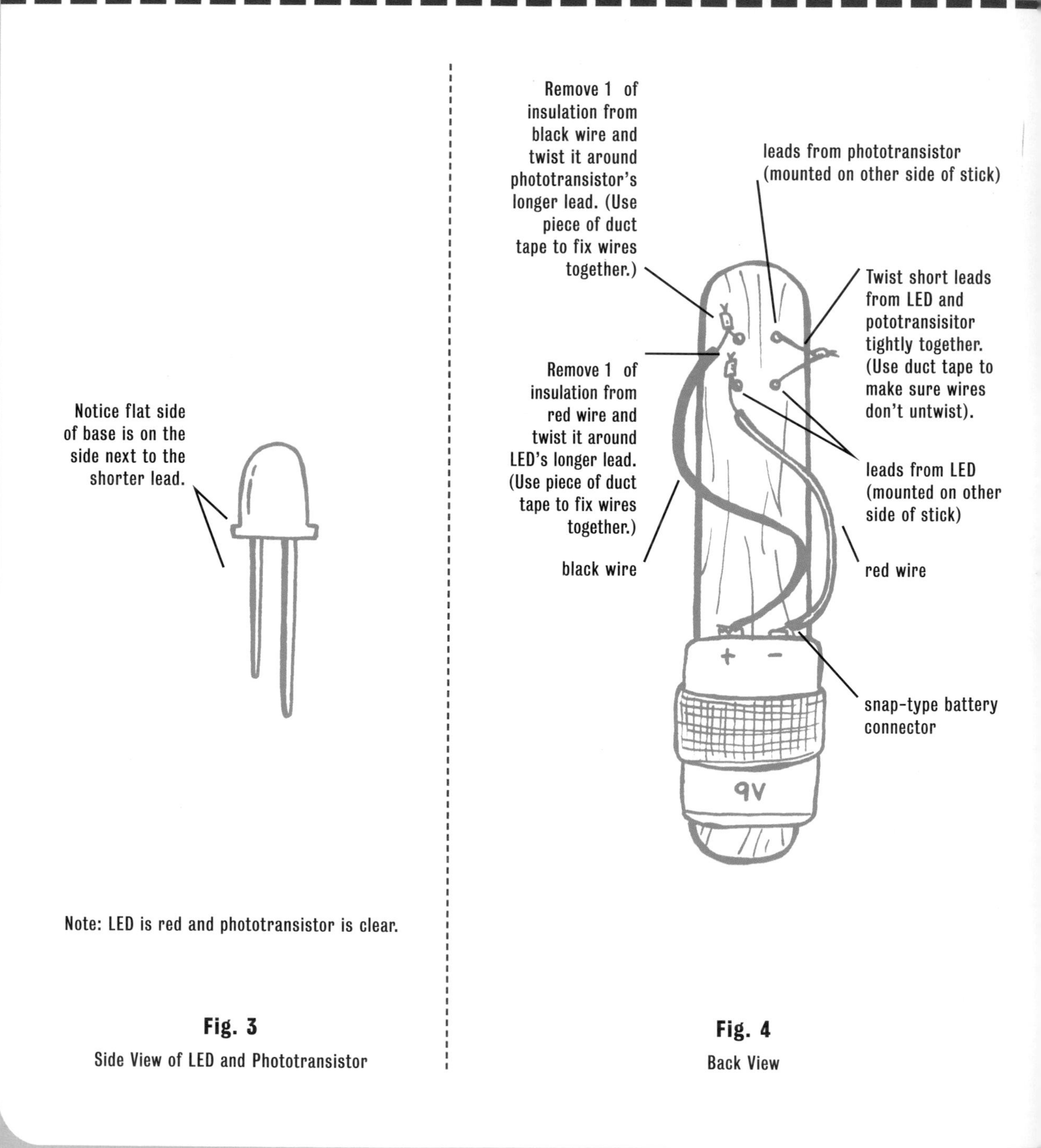


**Fig. 3**

Side View of LED and Phototransistor

**Fig. 4**

Back View

## AN AMAZING MAGIC TRICK

In addition to its practical use, the Sidewinder Thingamajig is the perfect prop for a neat magic trick. Place the Sidewinder Thingamajig near you. Tell your friends you're able to turn on the LED by just staring at it! They'll naturally look toward the LED. When the light amazingly goes on, challenge a friend to do the same. Of course, no matter how hard your friend stares at the LED, it won't go on! The trick you have up your sleeve, the remote control, is actually up your sleeve. When you press a button on the remote, the LED goes on! Make sure to turn the phototransistor so it will be easy for the invisible light beam to hit it.

Tips: Try this trick in the dark. The darkness increases the effect when the LED goes on. It will also make it nearly impossible for your friends to discover the remote control hidden in your sleeve. Make sure you wear a long-sleeve shirt and try it out a few times by yourself first!

## SAVING THE BATTERY

When you're not using the Sidewinder Thingamajig, it's best to take off the battery connector. You can also save the battery by keeping the phototransistor dark by placing the Sidewinder Thingamajig in a drawer or pocket.

# MAGICAL ELECTRICITY SENSOR

Project 16

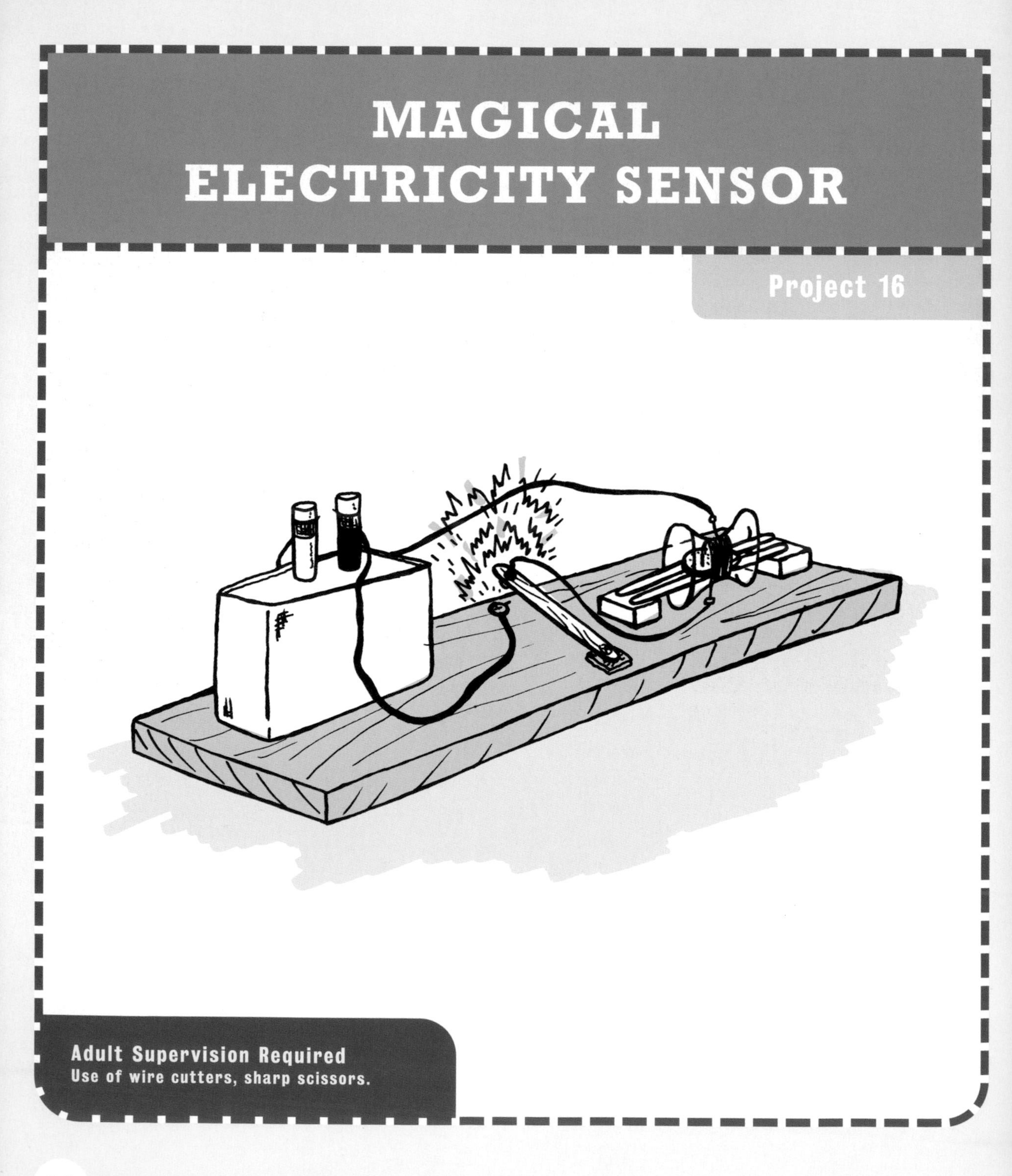

**Adult Supervision Required**
**Use of wire cutters, sharp scissors.**

In 1820, the Dutch scientist Hans Christian Oersted tried to show a class of students that electricity and magnetism were completely different. This was the prevailing belief at the time. He placed a compass near a wire that had electricity flowing through it. As he expected, the compass's needle didn't move. At one point, while Hans wasn't looking, a student turned the compass so its needle was at a right angle to the wire. When the electrical switch was turned on again, the compass's needle spun wildly. Bingo! Proof that electricity does create magnetism after all!

Making a sensitive instrument that detects electricity is easy. This one can even detect electricity from a battery made from a lemon!

## WHAT YOU NEED

- one good compass
- 50' of 26- or 30-gauge magnet wire
- 2' to 3' of regular plastic-coated hookup wire
- one 20-ounce or ½"-liter plastic soft-drink bottle
- one wood board
- a couple of small interlocking plastic building blocks
- three craft sticks
- three small wood screws
- one machine screw with washer and nut
- duct tape
- one small piece of foam packing material
- craft stick switch (see **Fig. 2**)

## 1 MAKING IT

1. As shown in **Fig.** 1, for the sensing unit wind the magnet wire around the plastic cut from an empty plastic soda bottle. Leave about a foot free at both ends.
2. Use sandpaper to remove the enamel from these ends so you can make good connections to the hookup wires.
3. Use small pieces of duct tape to hold the ends of the wires together to make good contact.
5. Make a craft stick switch (see **Fig.** 2).
4. Finally, use a pen to make an R on the board where shown in **Fig.** 3.

## 2 USING IT

Try out your electricity detector by connecting a flashlight battery in place of the homemade battery shown in **Fig.** 3. Before connecting the battery, be sure to turn the detector so that one end of the needle points at the letter R.

## 3 VINEGAR-SALT BATTERY

Now that you know how to make and use the Magical Electricity Sensor, let's see how to make your own electricity!

**WHAT YOU NEED**

- 1 cup of vinegar
- ¼" cup salt
- warm water to nearly fill container
- one old plastic container
- one piece of scrap galvanized pipe (any size)
- one length of scrap copper tubing (any size)
- duct tape

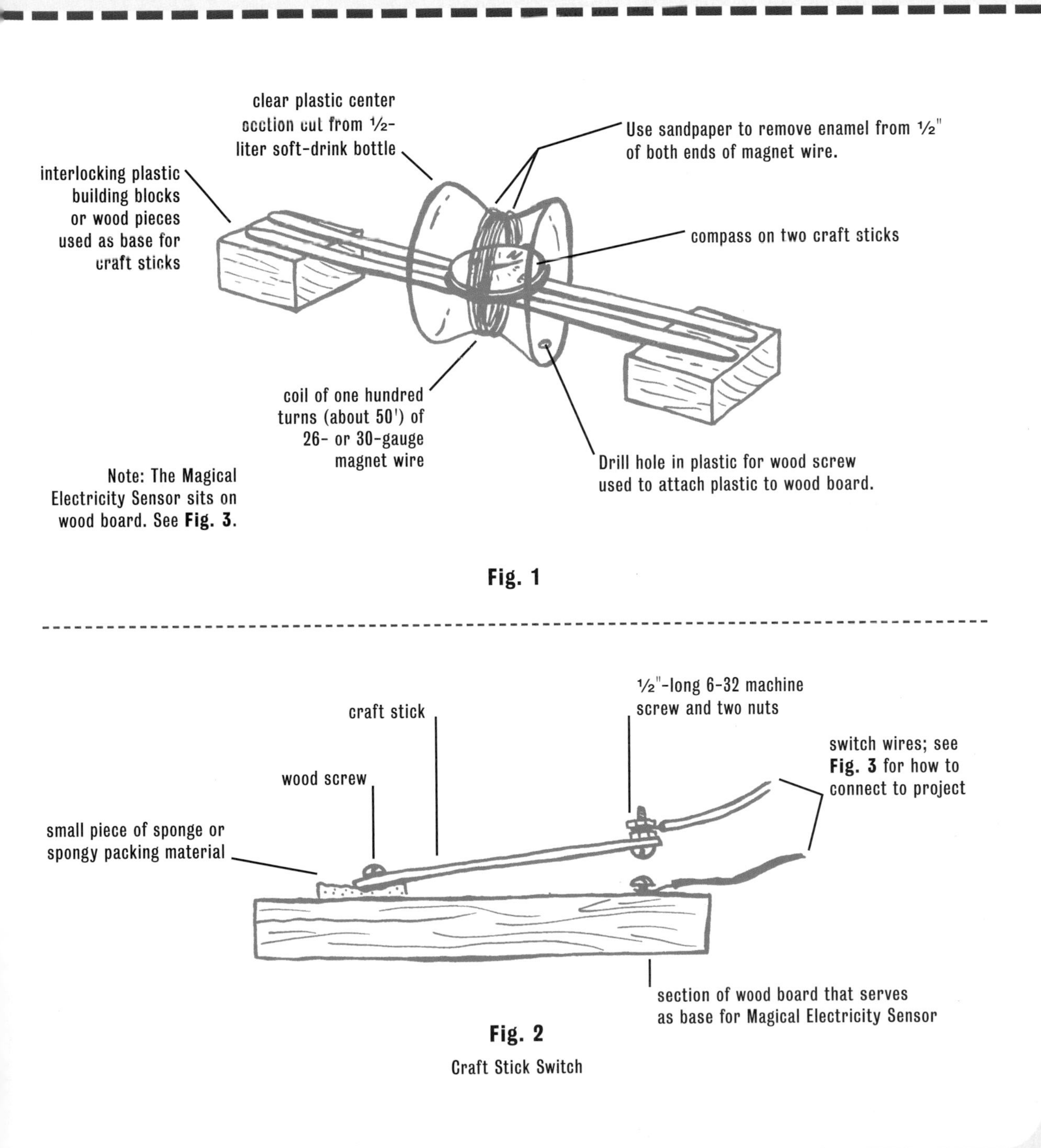


**Fig. 1**



**Fig. 2**

Craft Stick Switch

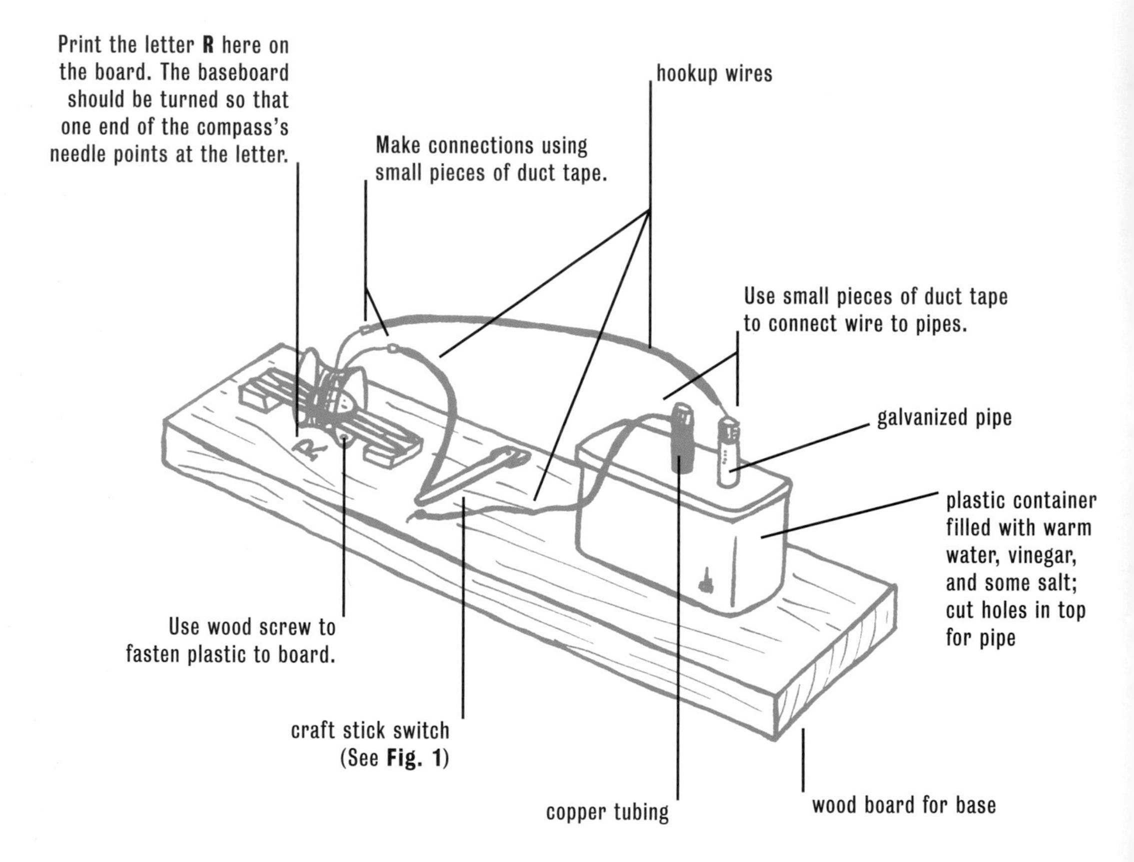
Print the letter **R** here on the board. The baseboard should be turned so that one end of the compass's needle points at the letter.
hookup wires
Make connections using small pieces of duct tape.
Use small pieces of duct tape to connect wire to pipes.
galvanized pipe
plastic container filled with warm water, vinegar, and some salt; cut holes in top for pipe
Use wood screw to fasten plastic to board.
craft stick switch (See **Fig. 1**)
copper tubing
wood board for base

**Fig. 3**

To make this homemade vinegar-salt battery, use **Fig. 3** as a guide. If you make it just right, this type of battery will create enough electricity to spin the compass's needle every time you press down on the craft stick switch!

Another, even easier-to-make, battery uses a large galvanized nail, a piece of heavy copper wire, and a lemon. Simply stick the nail and copper wire into the lemon and connect the wires to your detector! The "lemon battery" should be able to make the detector's needle turn a bit. The vinegar-salt battery will turn the needle a lot more. This is because it produces much more electricity than the lemon battery.

**ZINC**

**Zinc is a cheap, common, but mysterious metal. It doesn't rust, and so it is often used to coat steel. We call steel coated with zinc "galvanized steel."**

**Zinc is also used in many electric gadgets and in most batteries. Why is zinc mysterious? Well, tests have shown that when a battery is connected to a piece of zinc, positive charges flow through the zinc. However, according to most encyclopedias, electricity consists of the flow of tiny particles called electrons. We have known for years that electrons are negatively charged, not positively charged! While many scientists believe they can explain this apparent mystery, others are still fascinated by it.**

# MORSE CODE TELEGRAPH

Project 17

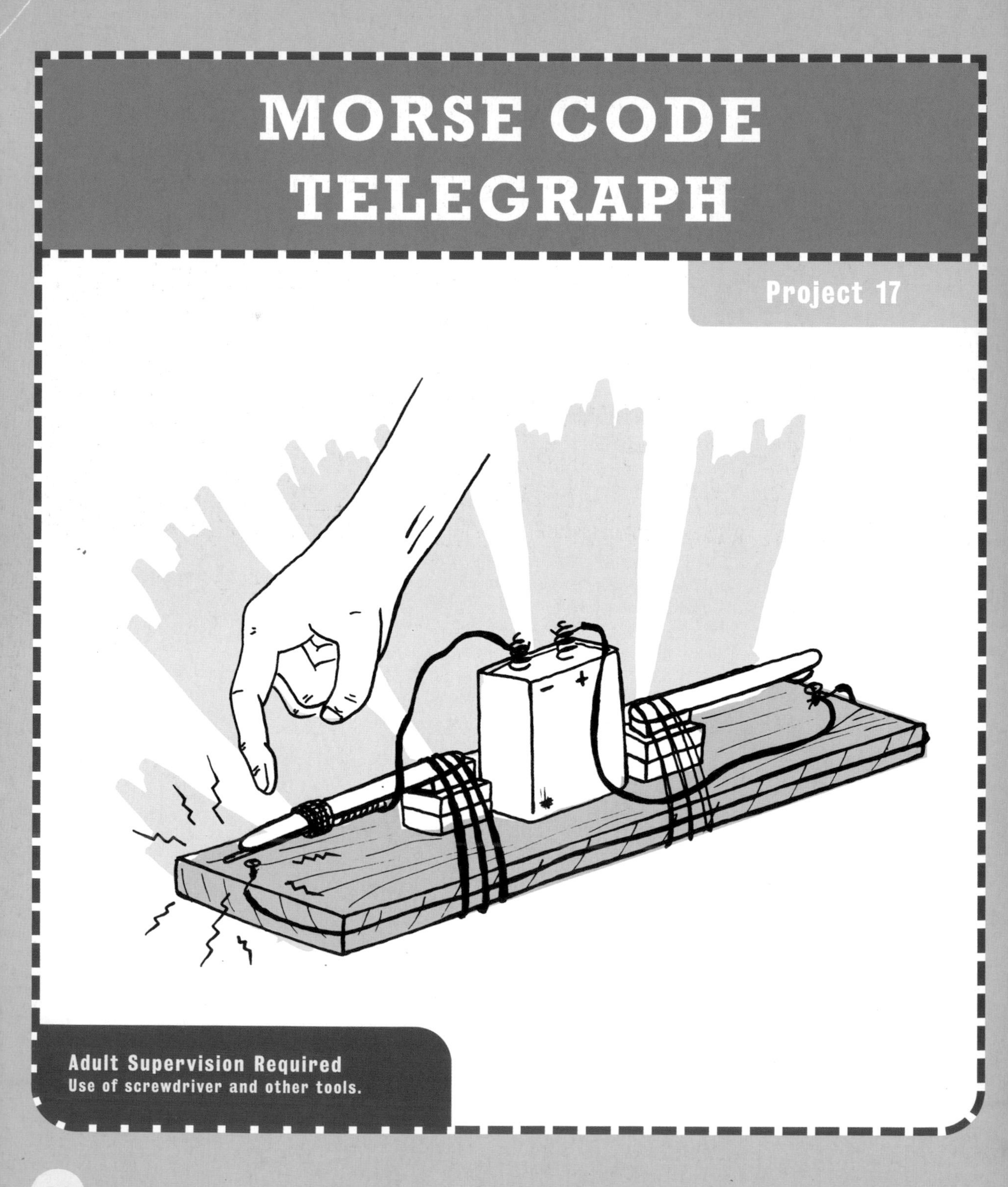


**Adult Supervision Required**
**Use of screwdriver and other tools.**

What on earth is this? Do these strange marks come from a piece of metal from an alien spaceship? Is it a message? Enough! It's time for answers. No, the marks aren't from an alien spaceship. Yes, there is a message. But what does it say?

## WHAT YOU NEED

- one 6-volt lantern battery
- one 16"–20" length of scrap 2 × 4 lumber
- interlocking plastic building blocks
- two craft sticks
- one steel washer
- six rubber bands
- two #10 1½" wood screws
- about 10' of #24 or #26 magnet wire
- about 3" of #14 copper wire, or a 2"–3" aluminum or galvanized nail
- about 3' of wire of any size as long as it has some insulation
- duct or adhesive tape
- double-sided tape
- one small nail

# 1 MORSE CODE

The telegraph was the first electrical device to make it possible to communicate over long distances, but only dots, dashes, and spaces could be transmitted that way. The code used by telegraph operators was named after the inventor of the telegraph, Samuel Morse.

The original code used in sending telegraph messages was known simply as Morse code. Then a slightly different code was developed, known as International Morse Code (see page 101). Use it to decode the "secret" message, which, by the way, is the first-ever recorded message sent cross-country by Morse telegraph.

1. Using **Fig.** 1 as a guide, use a nail to make a hole to start the wood screws.
2. To make the electromagnet, wind about 10' of magnet wire around one screw as shown.
3. Make the electrical connections by twisting two or three bare wires together with pliers. Duct tape can be used to keep the wires together. Before you make the connections, make sure the shiny copper in the wires is exposed. For plastic-coated wire, use either side cutters or a pair of scissors to remove about ½" of plastic on each end of the wire. With magnet wire, use fine sandpaper to remove about ½" of enamel at the two ends of the wire.

Use enough interlocking plastic building blocks so that there is roughly ¼" space between the top of the screw and the bottom of the wire or washer. Turn the screws to adjust this height.

# 2 SENDING SECRET MESSAGES

Once your "telegraph" is working, every time you press down on the sender's stick, causing the wire to touch the screw, you should hear a click in the receiver. A dot is made by a quick press. A dash is about twice as long as a dot. A space is three to four times as long as a dot and is placed between the end of one word and the beginning of the next word.

# 3 HOOKING UP TWO UNITS

If you make two units, you can communicate with a friend in another room. See **Fig.** 2. Telephone cable can be used to connect the two units. Use only the cable's red, black, and green wires. For lengths over 50', use either heavier wire or two batteries connected in series. See **Fig.** 3.

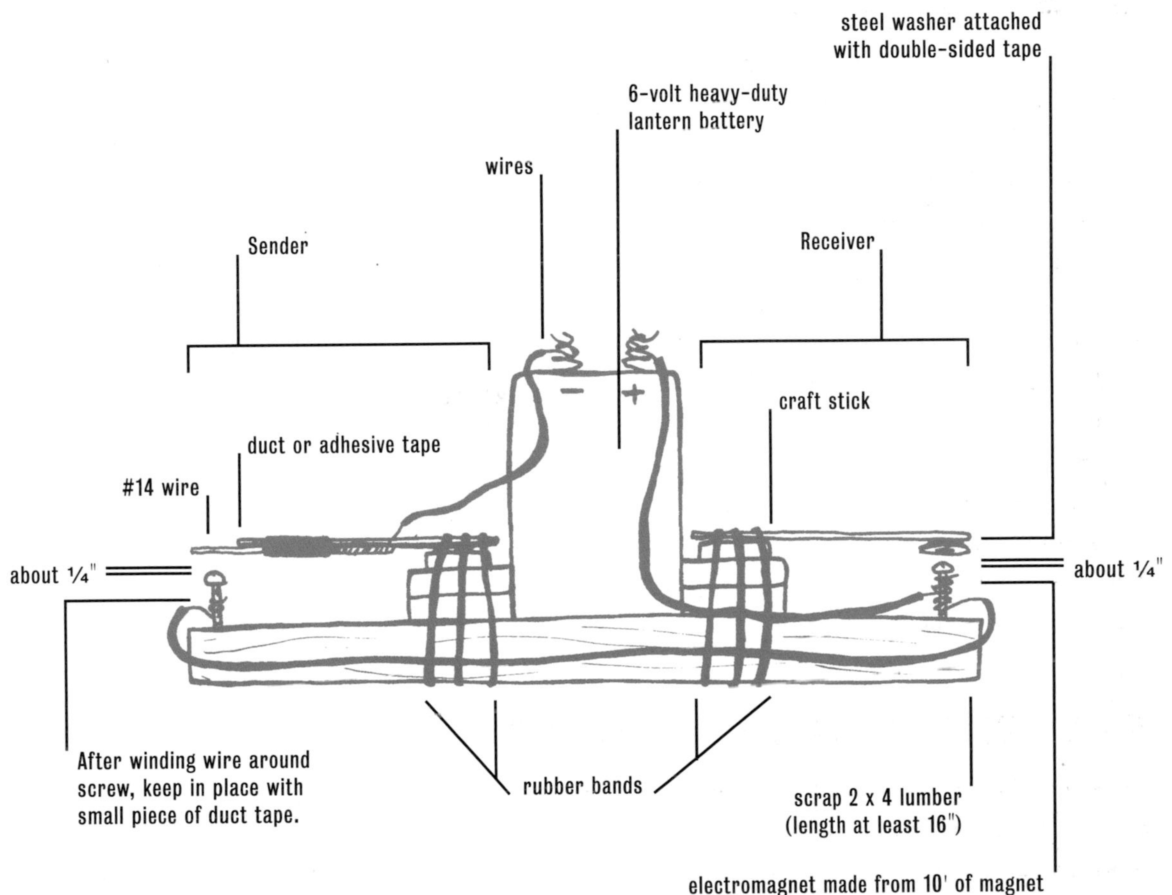
steel washer attached
with double-sided tape
6-volt heavy-duty
lantern battery
wires
Sender
Receiver
−
+
craft stick
duct or adhesive tape
#14 wire
about 1/4"
about 1/4"
After winding wire around
screw, keep in place with
small piece of duct tape.
rubber bands
scrap 2 x 4 lumber
(length at least 16")
electromagnet made from 10' of magnet
wire wrapped around wood screw

**Fig. 1**

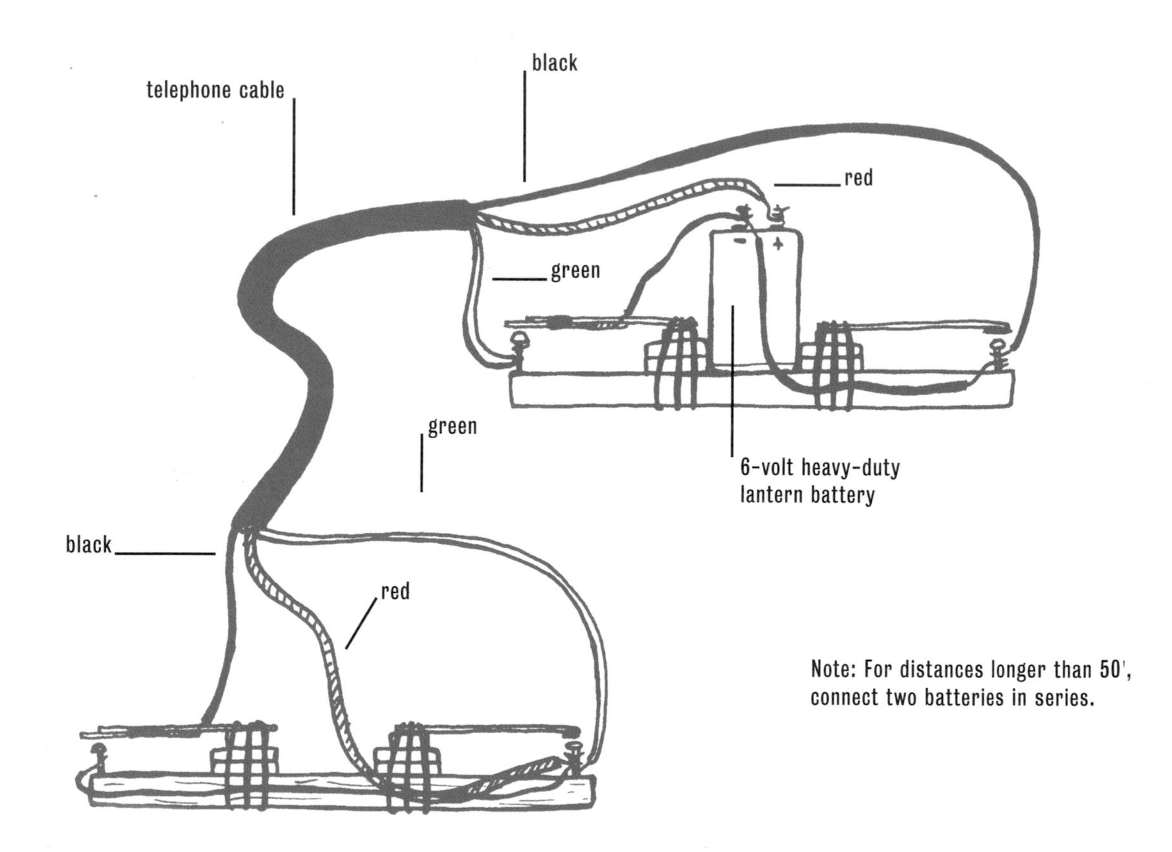


Note: For distances longer than 50', connect two batteries in series.

**Fig. 2**

Connecting Two Telegraph Units Together

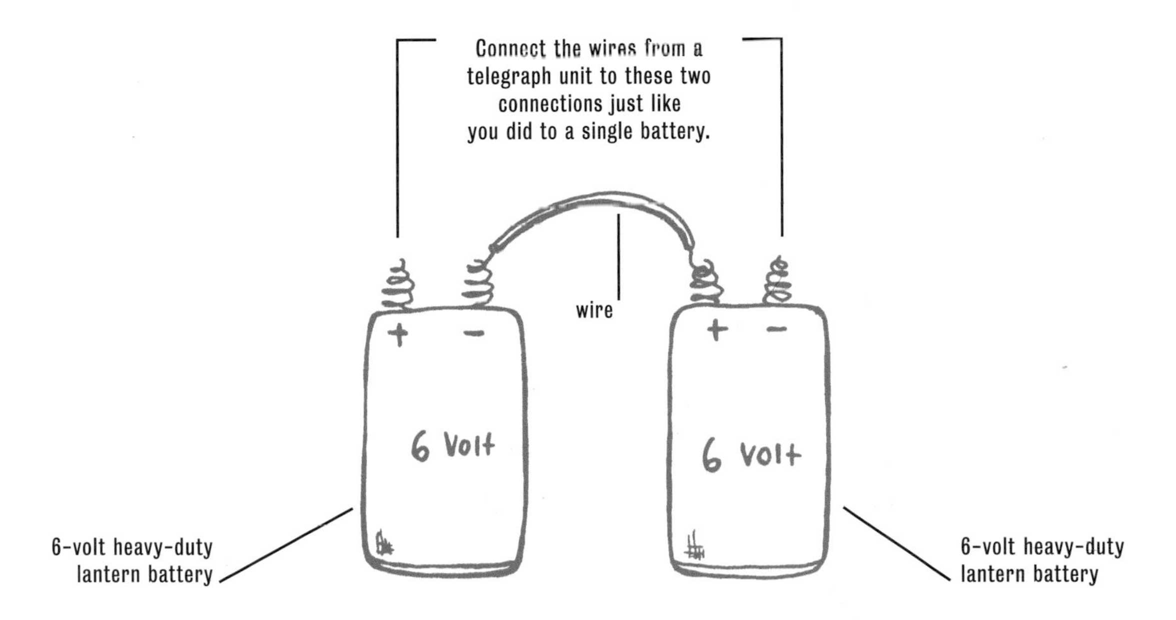


When you connect two batteries in series, the telegraphs can be used over longer distances.

**Fig. 3**

## International Morse Code

| | | | | |
|---|---|---|---|---|
| A • — | I • • | Q — — • — | Y — • — — | 6 — • • • • |
| B — • • • | J • — — — | R • — • | Z — — • • | 7 — — • • • |
| C — • — • | K — • — | S • • • | 0 — — — — — | 8 — — — • • |
| D — • • | L • — • • | T — | 1 • — — — — | 9 — — — — • |
| E • | M — — | U • • — | 2 • • — — — | full stop • — • — • — |
| F • • — • | N — • | V • • • — | 3 • • • — — | comma — — • — — |
| G — — • | O — — — | W • — — | 4 • • • • — | query • • — — • • |
| H • • • • | P • — — • | X — • • — | 5 • • • • • | |

# SECRET DRAWER LOCK

Project 18

**Adult Supervision Required**
Use of drill and tools

Secret passages and secret rooms are things that make certain movies and stories so much fun. While your house probably doesn't have a secret passage or room, you can make yourself something almost as neat—an electromagnetic secret drawer lock! This fun gizmo doesn't use a regular key to open it! What's the secret? Read on and you shall discover!

## WHAT YOU NEED

- one 6-volt lantern battery
- 75' #26 magnet wire
- one 3"-long ⅜" steel bolt
- one 3" length of ½" plastic PVC water pipe
- two 1½"-long 8-32 machine screws
- four 8-32 machine screw nuts
- one 5" length of a 1 × 4 wood board
- two 1¼"-long #8 wood screws
- one 1½"-wide by 5"-long piece of thin metal
- short length of elastic thread (can be from old clothing)
- duct tape

## 1 HOW IT WORKS

When electricity flows through a wire, magnetism is produced. That's all you really need to know! A plastic pipe is wound with about three hundred turns of magnet wire. Inside this pipe is a steel bolt with an elastic thread attached. This elastic thread pulls the bolt up when no electricity is supplied and keeps the drawer from being opened. When electricity flows through this wire, a magnetic field is created that pulls down the steel bolt. The drawer can then be opened!

## 2 MAKING IT

1. The first step in making the secret door lock is finding a drawer that is made out of wood. Check with your parents first.
2. Wind about three hundred turns of #26 magnet wire over the ½" plastic water pipe as shown in **Fig. 1**. Use duct tape to keep the wire in place. Leave about 8" of wire free at both ends.
3. Use sandpaper to remove the insulation from 1" of each end of the wires.
4. Also as shown in **Fig. 1**, tape a length of elastic thread to the bolt. Tape the other end of this thread to the outside of the pipe, as shown in **Fig. 2**.
5. Drill two 3⁄32" holes in a 5" by 1½" piece of thin metal, as shown in **Fig. 2**.
6. Lay the secret latch down on a 5" length of a 1 × 4 wood board and bend the metal over the latch. This metal will hold the latch to the board.
7. With a pencil, through the holes, make a mark on the

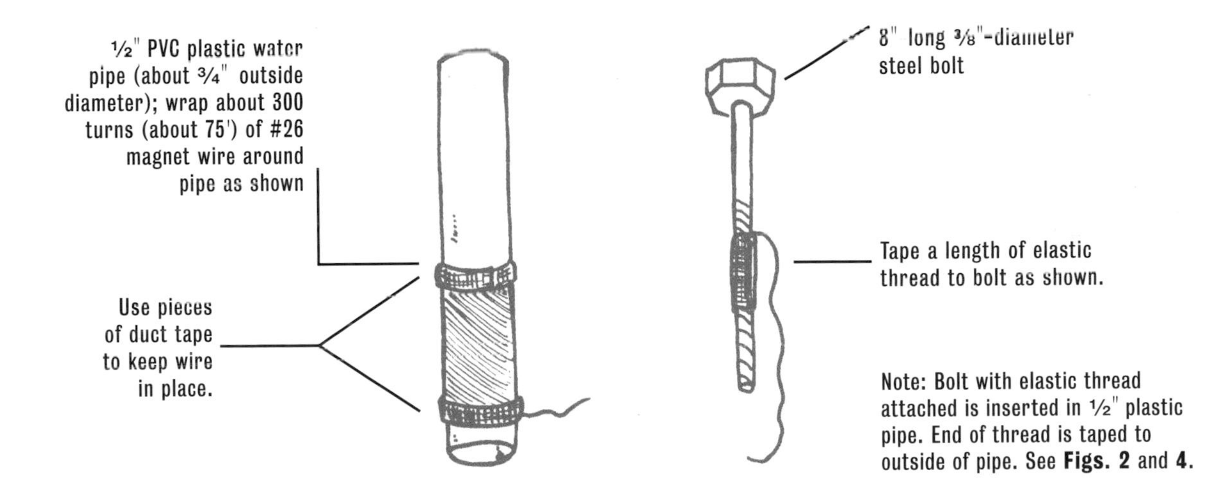


**Fig. 1**

Details of the Secret Drawer Lock's Construction

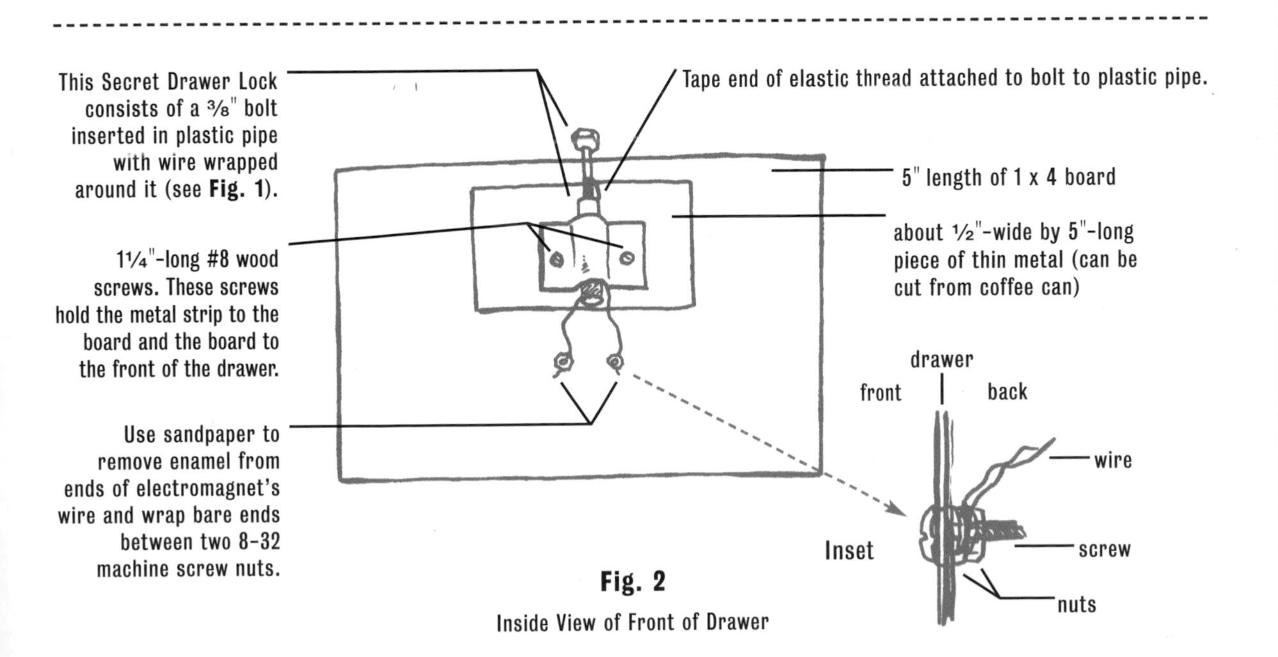


**Fig. 2**

Inside View of Front of Drawer

board. Drill ⅛" holes through the board using these pencil marks as a guide.

8. As shown in **Figs.** 2 and 4, use two 1¼"-long #8 wood screws to attach the electromagnet latch to the inside of the front of the drawer. Tighten the screws so that the thin metal holds the secret latch firmly to the drawer.
9. Drill two 3/32" holes in the drawer exactly 1" apart. Screws will be placed in these holes. These screws are the "secret" to opening the drawer. The screws' exact location is up to you; **Fig.** 3 is just a guide.
10. Insert two 1½"-long 8-32 machine screws in these holes. As shown in the inset in **Fig.** 2, firmly screw on one 8-32 nut to hold each screw and then loosely screw on another nut. Wrap the ends of the wires between the two nuts. Tighten the outside nut.

**Fig.** 3 shows the outside of the drawer. Notice the two machine screws. To open the drawer, press the lantern batteries' contacts onto the two screws and pull out the drawer. To close the drawer, either push the bolt down with your finger while closing it or use the battery. If you wish, you can add additional "phony" screws to make it even harder for someone to figure out the secret.

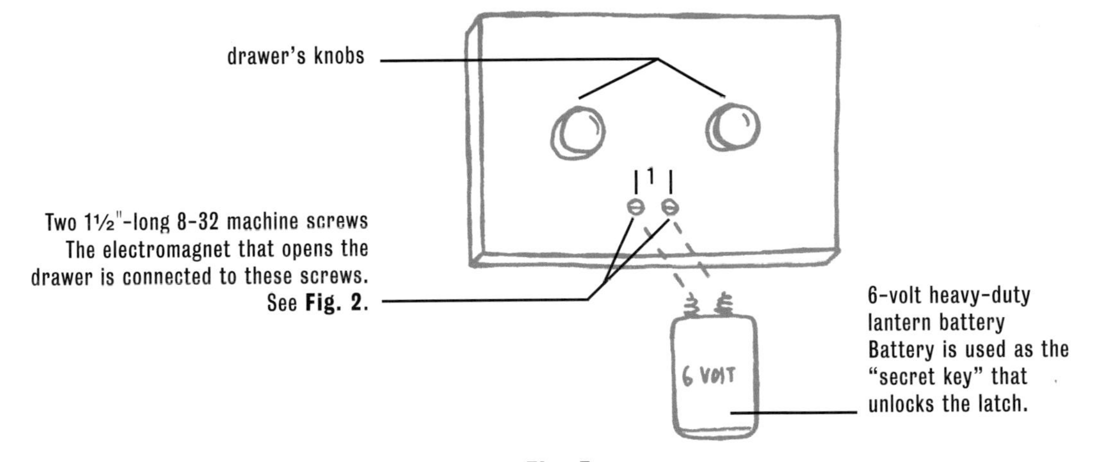


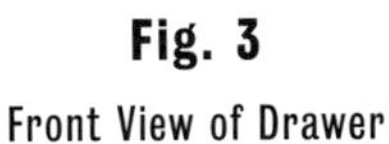

**Fig. 3**

Front View of Drawer

Normally, the elastic thread keeps the bolt pushed up so that the drawer can't be opened. When a battery is connected to the two front screws, the electromagnet is powered, which then pulls down the bolt, and bingo! The door can be opened!

**Fig. 4**

Inside View of Drawer Showing Secret Door Lock

BUILD-IT ROBOT
Project 19
Adult Supervision Required
Use of drill, saw, other tools.

Robots are fascinating. While we often think of them as movie special-effect gimmicks, the fact is that machines called robots have been around for many years, and they are finally coming closer and closer to what Hollywood and our imaginations have come to expect.

## WHAT YOU NEED

- two 6- to 13-volt DC electric motors (See note on DC electric motors, p. 113.)
- two heavy-duty rubber bands, ½" wide and 4" long
- one 12" × 6" piece of ⅜" plywood (This is the minimum size; maximum size is 17" × 9".)
- two 1½"-long lengths of a 1 × 4 wood board (motor support boards)
- one 2"-long length of a 1 × 6 wood board (caster support board)
- two ½" × ¾" × 5½" wood boards (a ½"-wide slice cut off a 1 × 6 board) (outside bearings)
- two 3¾" plastic lids from jars (a 40-ounce peanut butter jar works)
- two 3⅜" plastic lids from jars (medium-sized peanut butter jars)
- six craft sticks
- one small furniture caster (used as front wheel)
- one switch (slide switch recommended)
- one 6-volt lantern battery (alkaline type preferred)
- six 2" round-headed 6-32 machine screws (two are used for wheels' axles)
- four ¾" 6-32 machine screws (for connections to motor's leads)
- fourteen 6-32 nuts
- six #6 washers
- seventeen ⅜" #6 wood screws
- two ¾" #6 wood screws
- two female quick-disconnect connectors (needed only if motors have quick-disconnect connectors)
- insulated hookup wire
- duct tape, epoxy cement, petroleum jelly or machine oil, and plastic from an ice cream container (used as straps to hold down motors)

## 1 THE BIRTH OF MOTH-BOT

Have you ever looked at a streetlight on a warm summer evening? Did you notice a lot of flying insects circling around it? Many of the bugs are moths. They are attracted to the light. If you go on to add electronic smarts to the dumb robot described here, you will have a neat gadget—a Moth-Bot, which is our next project (Project 20). What does a Moth-Bot do? When it is dark, it just sits there and doesn't move. But if you shine a flashlight at it, it will come alive and move toward the flashlight. If you move the flashlight, the Moth-Bot will follow it!

But let's not get ahead of ourselves. You must first make a "dumb robot," one that is able to just move forward every time you flip its switch until it hits something. Then, in the next project, we will add some electronic smarts to that "dumb" robot, and turn it into Moth-Bot!

## 2 MAKING IT

The best way to tell you how to put together this complicated project is to show you. So this is how we'll do it.

1. Gather and prepare all the list of materials needed.
2. Go to each of the drawings (**Figs.** 1 to 11) and assemble what you need and see how things go together.
3. Select the tools you need, and get to work. Soon you'll be thinking like a construction engineer.

smaller lid
(about $3\frac{3}{8}$" diameter)
larger lid
(about $3\frac{5}{8}$" diameter)

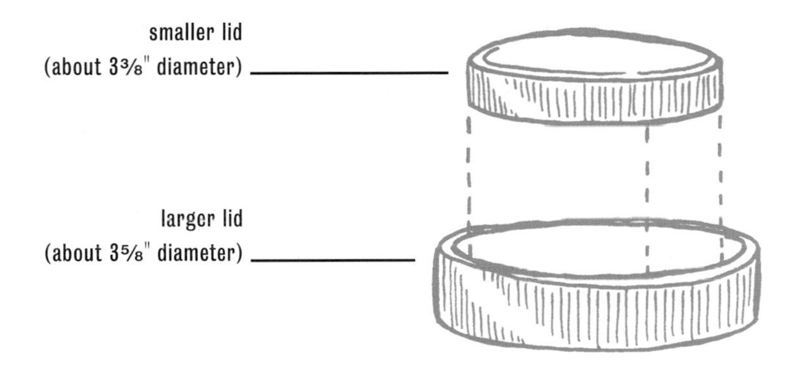

Stick smaller lid inside larger lid. This is done to make a stronger wheel.
Note: I used lids from large peanut butter jars, but lids from other containers can also be used.

**Fig. 1**

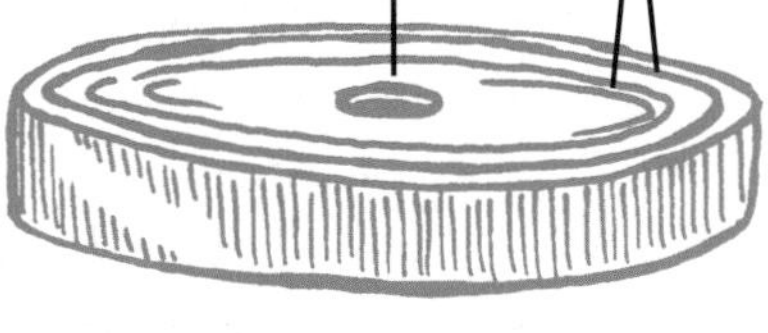

Drill a $\frac{1}{8}$" hole in the exact center of the wheel. You must drill through the top of both lids.
Note: Each wheel consists of two plastic lids. See also **Fig. 1**.

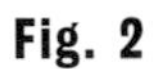

**Fig. 2**

## MY HERO

In 1984 I purchased a robot kit from Heathkit called HERO. It took many hours to put together, but it was worth it! The robot is really something! It can talk, move about, move one of its arms, and hear, and it has crude vision. It even has a kind of sound radar so that, even in pitch darkness, it knows when something is in front of it and how far away it is! By the way, HERO, which looks a bit like *Star Wars'* R2D2, made a cameo appearance in the sci-fi movie *The Last Starfighter*. Watch for him!

Created only as a gadget to help people learn about designing and using robots, HERO really can't do much that is useful. Today, many more practical robots are put to use in factories, but they usually do only a single task, such as welding or spray painting. These industrial robots don't look at all like movie robots, and very few can move about on their own.

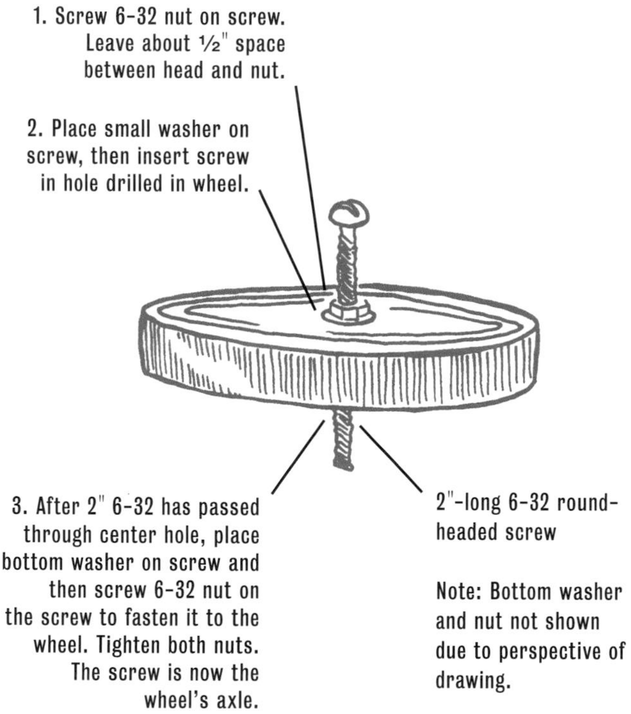

1. Screw 6-32 nut on screw. Leave about ½" space between head and nut.

2. Place small washer on screw, then insert screw in hole drilled in wheel.

3. After 2" 6-32 has passed through center hole, place bottom washer on screw and then screw 6-32 nut on the screw to fasten it to the wheel. Tighten both nuts. The screw is now the wheel's axle.

2"-long 6-32 round-headed screw

Note: Bottom washer and nut not shown due to perspective of drawing.

**Fig. 3**

# A LITTLE BIT ABOUT BEARINGS

Before getting into building the Build-It Robot, let's take a brief look at bearings and what they do. A bearing is part of a machine that guides and reduces the friction between a moving part and a part that doesn't move. Bearings are used in all types of machines that have parts that turn. Often, bearings are the "things" that go bad in machines that have something that turns a lot, like a wheel.

A simple bearing can be made by drilling a small hole in a wood board. If you stick a nail that is slightly smaller than the hole into this hole, the nail should be able to turn easily. To make it turn even more easily, place a drop of oil or a dab of petroleum jelly on the nail before sticking it through the hole. The wood with the hole is the "bearing" in this simple gizmo. Simple wood bearings will be used in this project.

**NOTE ON DC ELECTRIC MOTORS**

**The robot is propelled by two small DC motors. Don't use small slot-car motors or "toy motors"—they won't work well for this project. I tried several motor types before finding one that performed the way I wanted it to. Electronics outlets on the Internet often offer a number of motors that would be suitable, and orders from the website wouldn't incur a processing fee. You may also find there a wide range of robot parts and electronic components for similar type projects.**

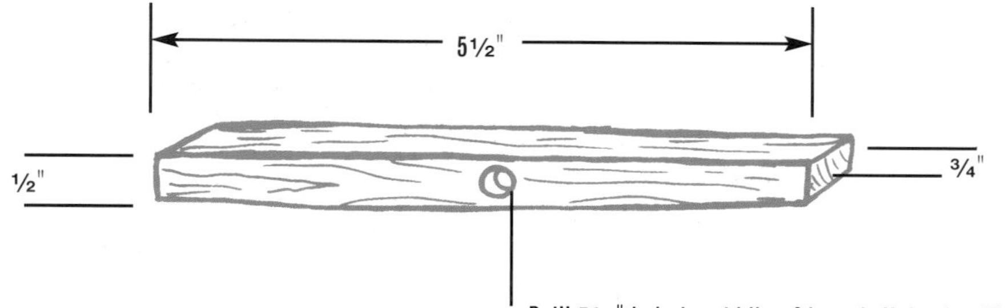


Drill 7/32" hole in middle of board. Hole should be between 3/8" and 1/2" deep. The head of the screw must be able to turn easily in this hole.

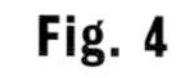

**Fig. 4**

outside bearing—two needed

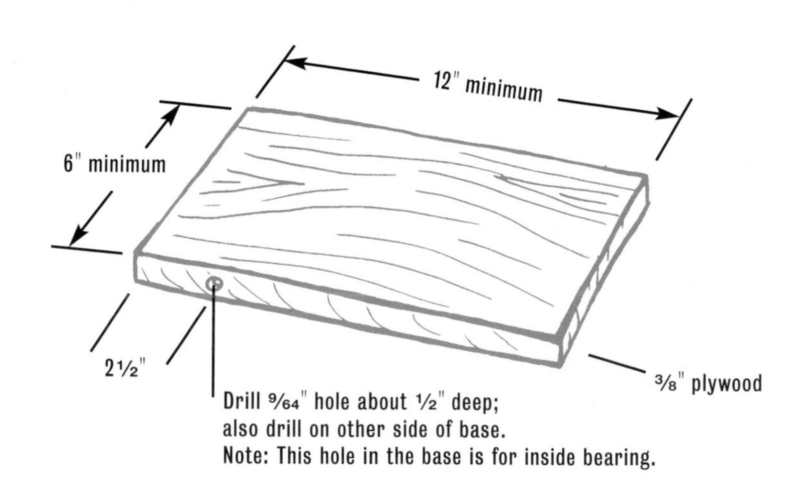

**Fig. 5**

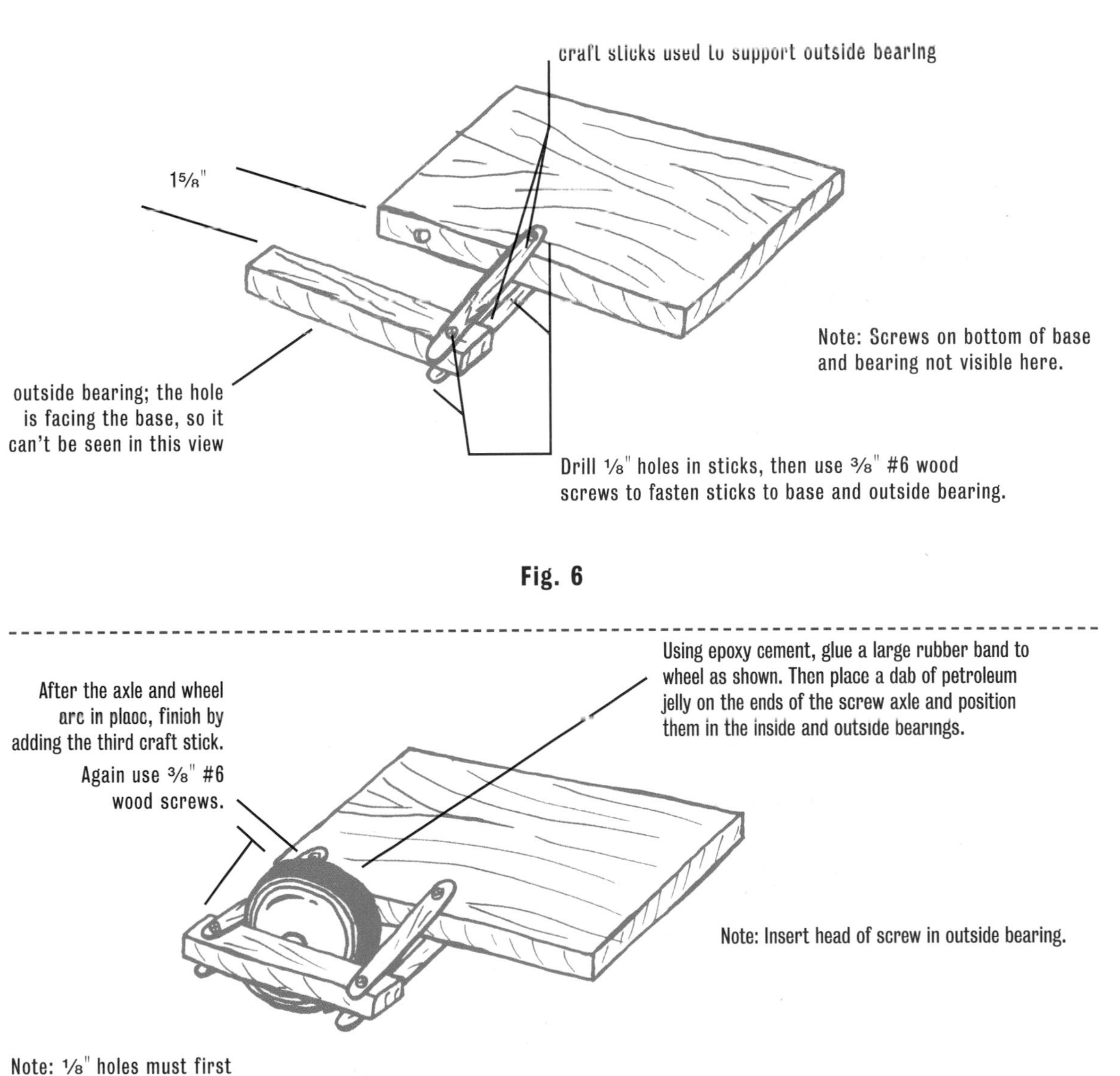
craft sticks used to support outside bearing
1 5/8"
Note: Screws on bottom of base and bearing not visible here.
outside bearing; the hole is facing the base, so it can't be seen in this view
Drill 1/8" holes in sticks, then use 3/8" #6 wood screws to fasten sticks to base and outside bearing.
Using epoxy cement, glue a large rubber band to wheel as shown. Then place a dab of petroleum jelly on the ends of the screw axle and position them in the inside and outside bearings.
After the axle and wheel are in place, finish by adding the third craft stick.
Again use 3/8" #6 wood screws.
Note: Insert head of screw in outside bearing.
Note: 1/8" holes must first be drilled in craft sticks.

Fig. 6

Fig. 7

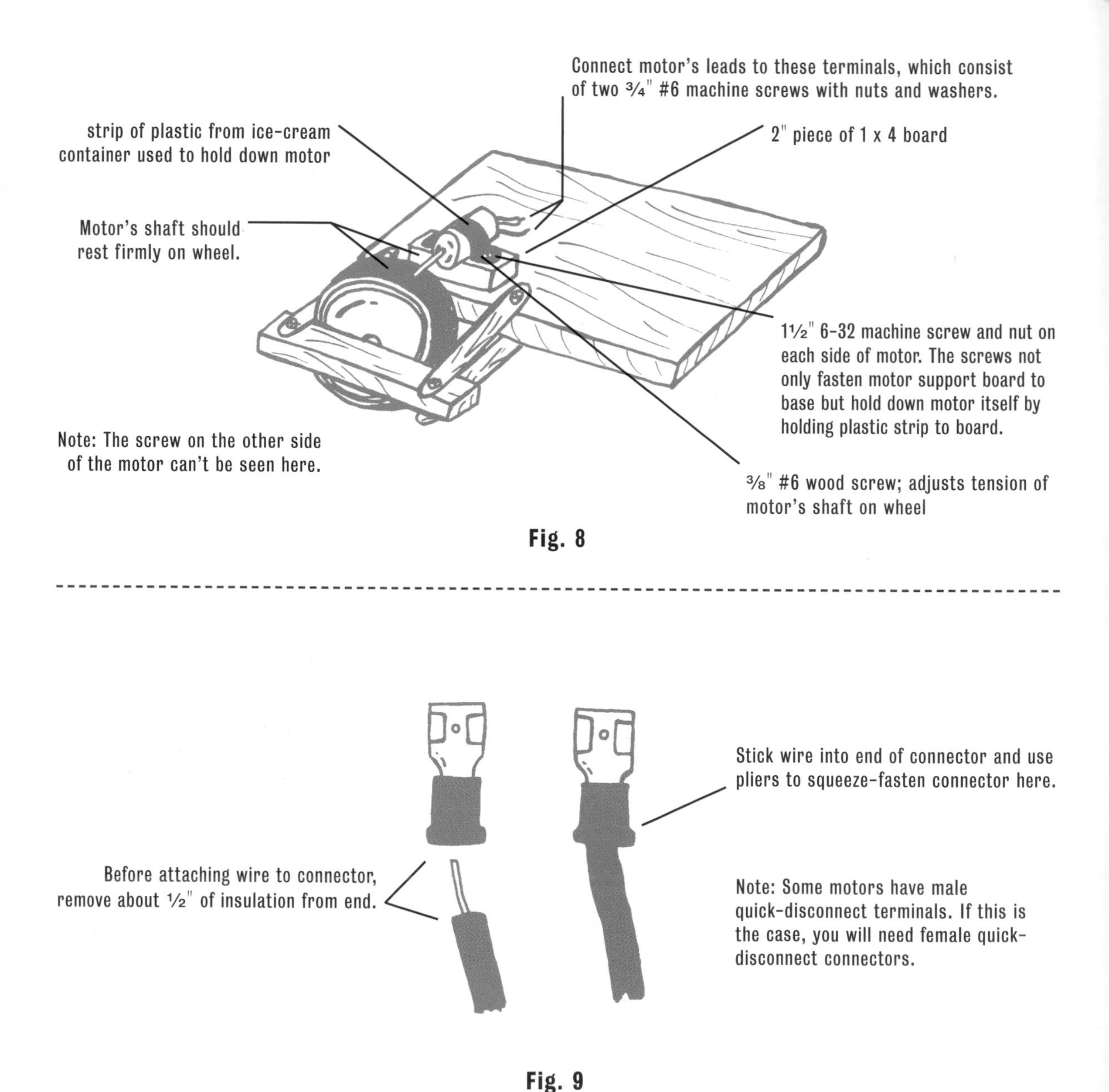


**Fig. 8**

**Fig. 9**

Attaching Wire to a Typical Female Quick-Disconnect Connector

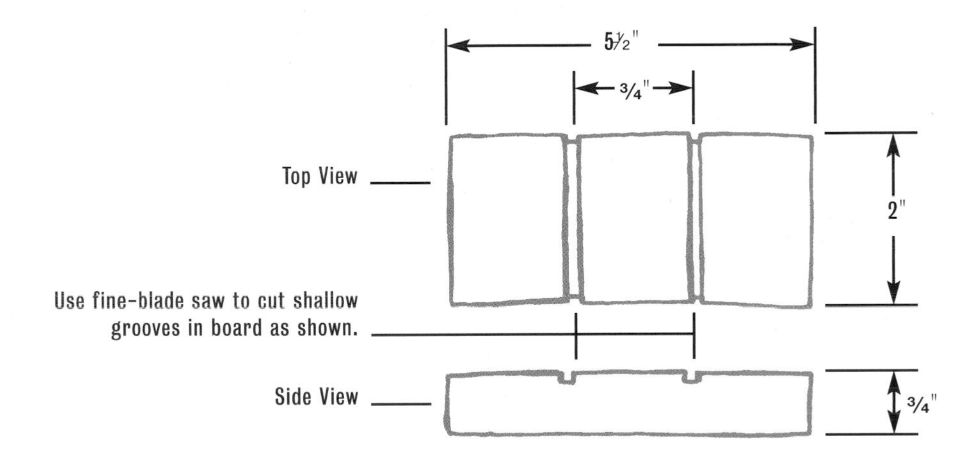

**Fig. 10**

Caster Support Board

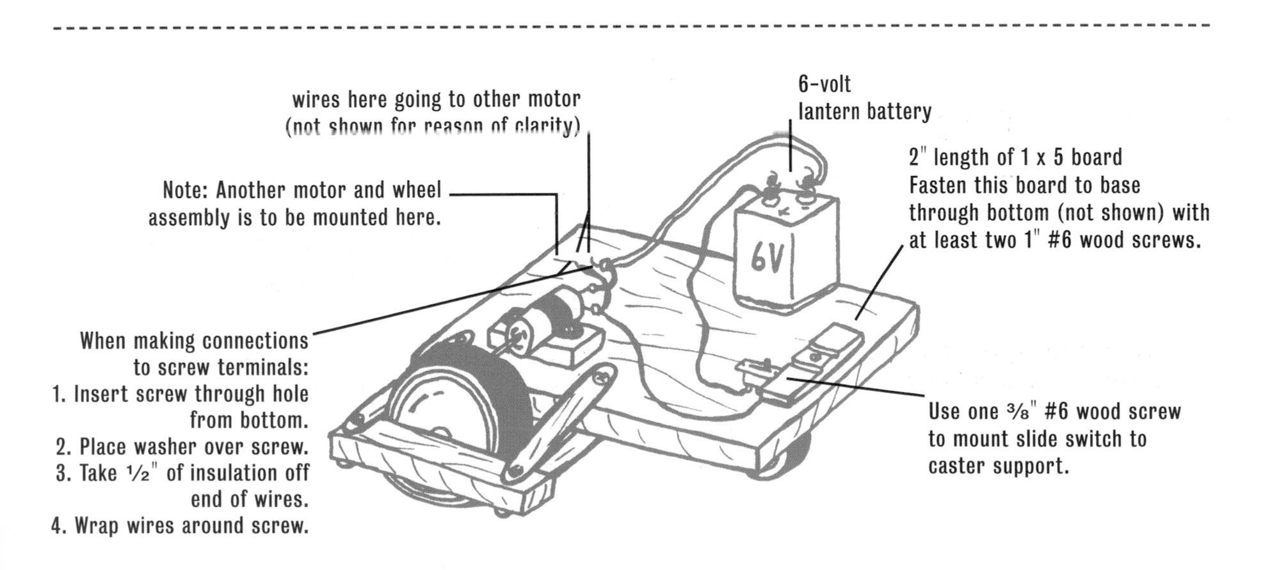


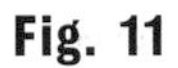
**Fig. 11**

# BRAIN-POWERED ROBOT

Project 20

**If you built the last project (Build-It Robot) and ran it on the floor, you quickly discovered how dumb it is—all it does is move forward until it hits something. This project will show you how to add a bit of smarts to the robot with a simple electronic circuit. If you run this Moth-Bot in a large room without obstructions or outside in the late evening on a hard surface, you will find it truly amazing.**

## WHAT YOU NEED

- one Build-It Robot (see Project 19)
- one modular IC breadboard socket
- two NPN phototransistors
- two NPN power transistors
- two NPN transistors
- 22-gauge solid insulated hookup wire
- two heat sinks*
- two 6-32 nuts
- cardboard
- wood glue
- duct tape

*A good, inexpensive heat sink can also be simply made from a 2" square of light aluminum sheeting (not foil).

## TRANSISTORS

Before describing how to actually add the smarts to the Build-It Robot, let us take a brief look at a transistor, which is the main electronic part used here. This project will be using six of these tiny, but amazing, electronic parts.

If you have ever looked through a magnifying glass you should be able to get an idea of what a transistor does. Instead of making stuff look bigger, like a magnifying glass does, a transistor magnifies electric current. One other point: We usually use the verb "amplify" rather than "magnify" when talking about electricity.

There is something else about transistors, other than the fact they amplify electricity—they are sensitive to light. Because of this, they are usually encased in a material that is opaque, which means light can't pass through it. Some types of transistors, however, are encased in clear plastic. These types of transistors are called phototransistors. When light strikes a phototransistor, it causes electric current to flow. When phototransistors are in total darkness, no significant electricity flows through them.

Each of the two motors in the Build-It Robot is controlled by three transistors. A phototransistor, which lets current through when light hits it, is connected to a regular transistor, which amplifies this current. This second transistor is connected to a power transistor, which actually controls the motor. While the power transistor also amplifies, its main purpose is to provide enough current to run the motor. Because so much current flows through the power transistor, it can become warm.

## WIRING DIAGRAM

**Fig.** 2 is a wiring diagram that shows how one motor is controlled by a phototransistor. This drawing is meant only as a guide and to help you understand how the Moth-Bot works. Wires can be connected as shown in **Fig.** 2 by twisting them together and using duct tape, but it is smarter, and easier, to use the Experimenter Breadboard, which is described next.

## EXPERIMENTER BREADBOARD WIRING

1. The first step here is to remove all the wires from the Build-It Robot project (Project 19) except for the wire that goes from the A+ terminal of the battery to the switch and the wires that go from the motor to the screw terminals mounted on the base. *All other wires should be removed.*
2. Carefully follow **Fig.** 1, which shows an experimenter breadboard with the transistor's leads and

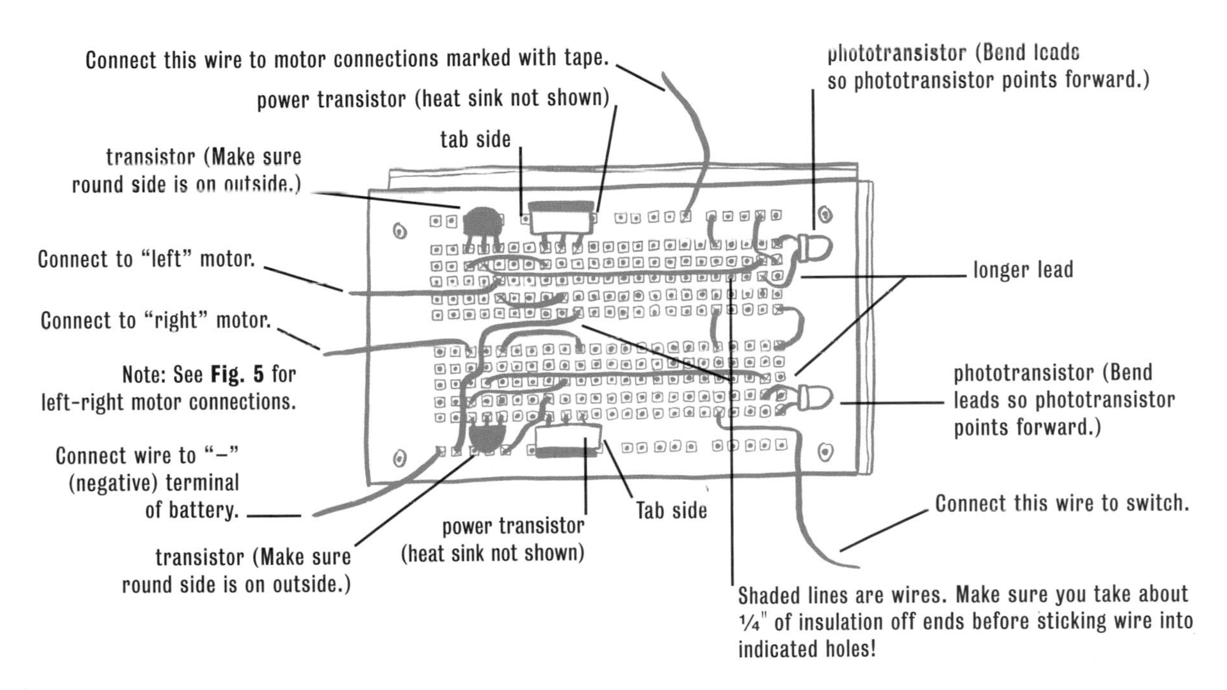


**Fig. 1**

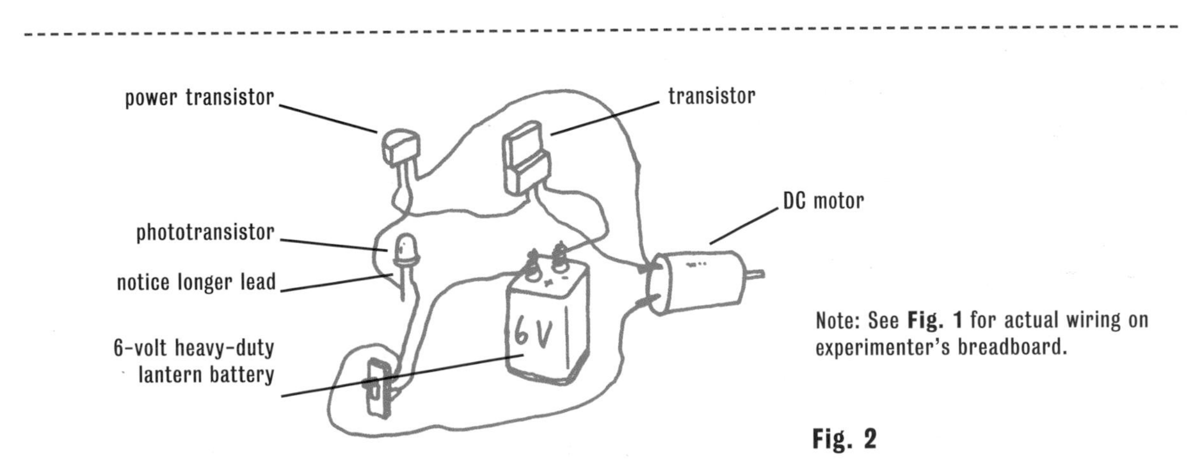


**Fig. 2**

Wiring Diagram for One Motor

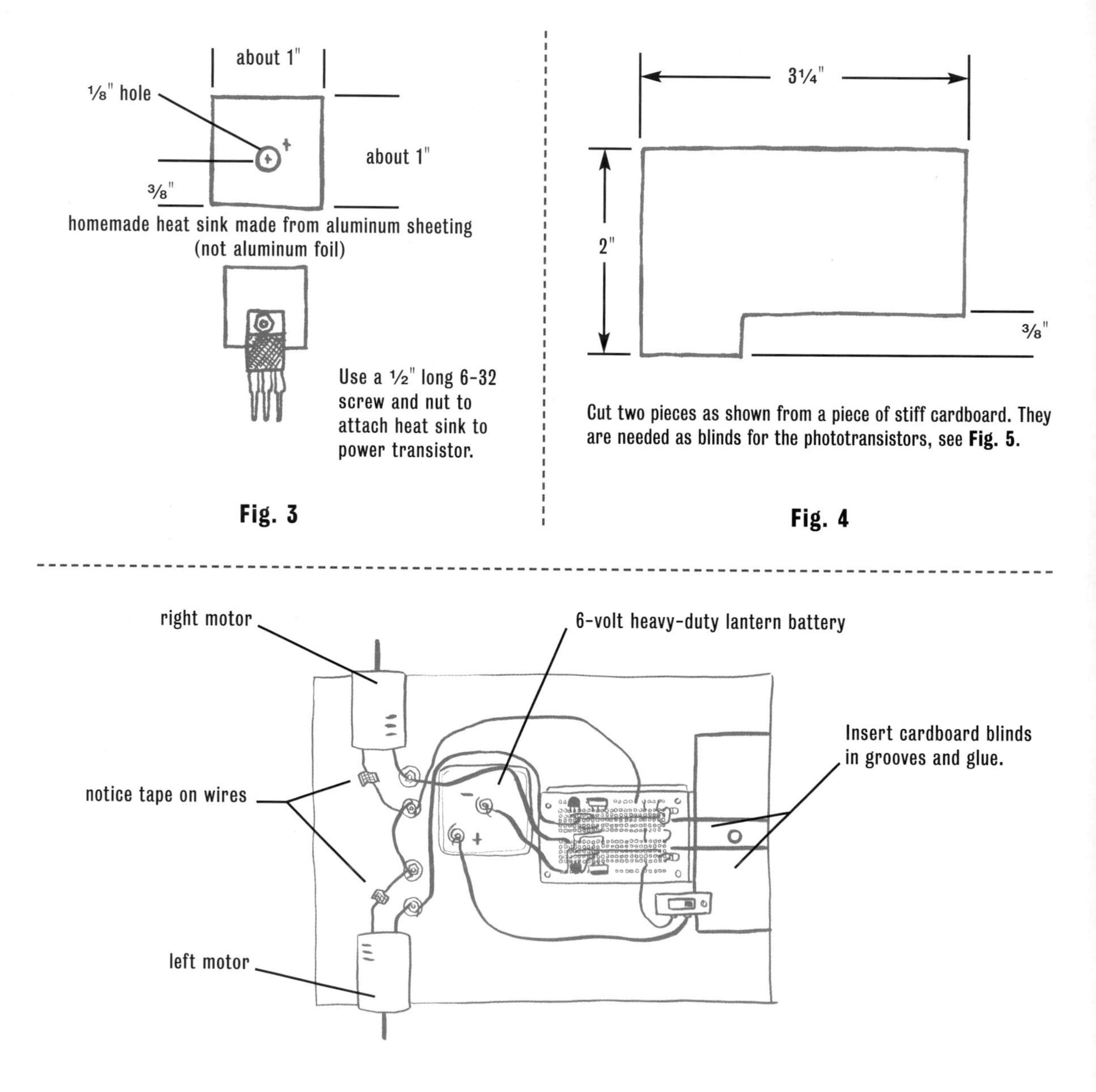


**Fig. 3**

Cut two pieces as shown from a piece of stiff cardboard. They are needed as blinds for the phototransistors, see **Fig. 5**.

**Fig. 4**

**Fig. 5**

wires inserted in it. Position the transistors exactly as indicated. Notice that one side of each small transistor is a flat side and the other side is rounded. Also notice that one lead of the phototransistor is longer than the other. Make sure you install the right lead in the right hole!

The wires in **Fig. 1** are shaded to help guide you in connecting the wires correctly. It isn't necessary for you to use different shades of wires—it just makes things a little easier and there is less chance of goofing up by connecting the wires to wrong holes or wrong parts.

3. Before you install the power transistors, use a ½" 6-32 screw and nut to fasten a heat sink to them. This heat sink can be one already made or you can make one yourself out of aluminum sheeting. See **Fig. 3** for details.
4. Install the phototransistors where shown on the breadboard.
5. Bend the phototransistors' leads down slightly as shown. Since the leads on the power transistors are fairly large, use care when pushing their leads into the holes in the breadboard.
6. Mount the breadboard to the base of the robot with two 1½"-long 6-32 screws and nuts. See **Fig. 5**. After mounting the breadboard to the base, check to make sure you haven't pulled out any wires or leads from the breadboard.
7. Now, referring closely to **Fig. 5**, wire the board into the circuit. Make sure you put the end of each wire in the correct hole and you connect the other end to the correct place. Notice that **Fig. 5** is a top view and is meant solely as a wiring aid. *Note:* **Fig. 5** leaves out some nonelectrical parts of the Build-It Robot.
8. Take heart! You are almost done, and very soon you will be able to throw the *big switch* and find out whether the Moth-Bot works! This final construction step is simple. First, fill the grooves in the caster support board with a tiny amount of wood glue.
9. Finally, cut two pieces of cardboard and glue the edges in the grooves in the caster support board. **Fig. 4** is the template for the cardboard blinds, and **Fig. 5** indicates where they are mounted. Note that it is best to use pliers to first flatten the edge of the pieces of cardboard that will be inserted in the caster support board's grooves.

## THROWING THE BIG SWITCH!

When you make electric stuff, the fun begins when you start putting the project together. However, the excitement begins when you near the finish and are anxious to turn the switch on to see whether it works! Why is this so exciting? Simple. You are not sure what will happen! Will you see sparks? Will the thingamajig just sit there and stare back at you and do nothing? Or will it do something you never thought it would—something you've never, ever seen a gadget do before? Or perhaps will it work just as you expected! This project is fairly complicated, so it is doubtful that it will work just right when you turn it on. However, as long as you finally get it to work, the fact that it doesn't work right the first time just makes the thrills last longer! Having it not work right away also teaches you patience. Anything really worthwhile is worth waiting for.

Before turning on the switch, make sure all the wires are connected to something and not just dangling. Put the Moth-Bot down on a hard-surfaced floor—not a carpet. Lay a piece of paper over the phototransistors so they "think" it is dark. Get a flashlight ready. Turn on the switch. Nothing should happen! Not a thing! Make sure the transistors aren't getting hot and the battery isn't getting warm. If anything gets really warm, turn off the switch and check all the wiring again.

If everything so far looks good, take the paper off the phototransistors. If neither motor turns, shine the flashlight on one or both phototransistors. With the flashlight shining on the left phototransistor, for example, the right motor should turn. If your Moth-Bot is working as it should, it is time for the real fun! But first, shut off the switch.

## RUNNING IT

Place your Moth-Bot on the hard-surfaced floor of the largest room you can find that has the fewest number of things in it to get in the way. (If you have a smooth-surfaced driveway or patio, you can try the Moth-Bot outside in the late evening or at night.)

Have a flashlight ready and shut off all the lights. You may need to pull down the shades or close the blinds, too. Turn on the switch. If the light in the room is dim enough, the Moth-Bot shouldn't move. Now, shine the light on a phototransistor. The Moth-Bot should start moving, turning toward the flashlight. As it moves and turns toward the light, the other motor should start up. The Moth-Bot should now move straight ahead, toward the light. Move the light again. The Moth-Bot should again turn toward the light. If it is nighttime and you put a small table lamp in the middle of the floor of a large room and turn off all the other lights, the Moth-Bot should be able to find its way to the lamp no matter where you put it in the room—as long as the Moth-Bot doesn't bump into something, that is.

## AN INTERESTING EXPERIMENT

If you know of a large, smooth, and level empty parking lot, you may want to try out an interesting experiment with your Moth-Bot. Just before sunset on a clear day, put the Moth-Bot at the east end of the parking lot and point it toward the southwest. Assuming the sun is setting in the west (it sets anywhere from the southwest to the northwest depending upon the time of year; only twice a year, at the start of spring and the start of fall, does it actually set due west), the Moth-Bot should start up and turn right until it "sees" the sun. It then should move pretty straight, directly at the setting sun. If everything goes as planned, the Moth-Bot should continue moving toward the setting sun, moving left and/or right at times to correct itself, until either the sun sets completely or the Moth-Bot hits something or gets stuck in some mud or gravel!

## SOME OTHER POSSIBILITIES

One of the hardest and trickiest parts of building a project like the Moth-Bot is to get it moving and turning reliably. As you saw, Project 19's Build-It Robot was harder to build than Project 20's adding of the "smarts," which consist primarily of wiring. With the addition of more electronic circuits, the Moth-Bot can do a lot more than just move toward a light! For instance, by adding a bare wire switch assembly to the front of the base and circuitry, likely consisting of two relays and several integrated circuits, a mechanism could be made that would make the Moth-Bot back up and turn every time it hit something. This would allow the Moth-Bot to continue to roam around looking for light even if there were things in the way that it could run into. Of course, you probably won't be able to make such a really smart Moth-Bot on your own, but maybe you know someone who could help you. Or this book may be all the encouragement you need to learn more about electricity and come up with your own electronic design to add any needed circuitry yourself!

# PROJECT NOTES

NOTE: DO NOT WRITE HERE – MAKE A PHOTOCOPY FOR EACH PROJECT AND KEEP PROJECT NOTES IN BINDER.

**PROJECT (NUMBER & NAME):** ______________________________

**DATE STARTED:** ______________ **DATE COMPLETED:** ______________

**Source of materials:** ______________________________

______________________________

______________________________

**Problems/adjustments made:** ______________________________

______________________________

______________________________

______________________________

**Improvements/modifications made:** ______________________________

______________________________

______________________________

______________________________

**Photos taken? If so, type and location:** ______________________________

______________________________

______________________________

**Additional notes:** ______________________________

______________________________

# INDEX

# ABOUT THE AUTHOR

TOM FOX is a well-known writer in the electronics and computer fields. He has been published in *Popular Electronics, Radio-Electronics, Elementary Electronics, Electronics Now, Modern Electronics, Hands-On Electronics, Microcomputer Journal,* and other publications. His interests and talents aren't limited to these technical subjects, though. Many of his numerous (over a hundred) articles have appeared in *Boys' Life, Hopscotch, Michigan Out-of-Doors, Coins, Mother Earth News,* and *BackHome.* He has also written a book of electronic weather projects and one on programming the HC11 microcontroller.

Tom Fox has a master of science degree in electrical engineering from the Illinois Institute of Technology and is currently the workshop editor at both *Boys' Quest* and *Fun for Kidz* magazines. He owns and operates, along with his family, Magicland Farms—a roadside farm market in Michigan. Information on the farm market and a contact information link for readers of this book can be found at Tom Fox's website: http://www.magiclandfarms.com.

Tom Fox lives with his wife and six children on a small lake not far from his farm and roadside farm market.